D1110430

thebrownbaglunchcookbook

MIRIAM JACOBS

The Globe Pequot Press

GUILFORD, CONNECTICUT

To Hedi ter Veer-Grün

who loved to cook

Text design: Nancy Freeborn
Photography: Chris Dube
Library of Congress Cataloging-in-Publication Data available
ISBN 0-7627-2758-6

Manufactured in the United States of America
First Edition/First Printing

Contents

Acknowledgments

I want to thank David Emblidge, acquisitions editor at The Globe Pequot Press, with whom I discussed the need for this book and who then took the lead to make it happen, and Cary Hull, project editor, whose patience saw this book through to the end. I thank my kids on whom I tried out my imaginative cooking and my boring sense of good nutrition. And thanks also to my mom, Selma Jacobs, without whom I might not have realized for a long time that fast food and vitamin pills do not constitute a balanced diet.

About This Book

Lunchtime ought to be an enjoyable break from work. To feel good, stay lively, and perform well for the balance of the day, we need a healthy lunch. The catch is that it has to be interesting and efficient too. The good news is, as you will see in this book, there are loads of convenient and economical homemade foods that will nourish you well, lots better than takeout fast food ever could.

The most common complaint is that "we don't have enough time." Our lives are so stressed and busy that finding the time for yet one more thing seems overwhelming. The recipes in this book have been put together with that very thought in mind; they are super fast as well as uncomplicated to make.

The ideal time to make lunch is when you are cleaning up from dinner, when you might be looking at some leftovers. This book gives you lots of ideas of how to incorporate them into a delicious lunch. Even if you don't have any leftovers, it is still a good time to make lunch because somehow, psychologically, it doesn't seem like such a big deal to dirty one more knife and make a few sandwiches and a quick salad. (I would recommend that you start making the next day's dinner then too, if you possibly can.) Batching all your cooking that way makes it a lot less stressful.

Don't look on these as diet recipes, and don't expect them to address specific allergy issues. (If you are allergic to wheat, eggs, or dairy you'll need to consult a cookbook that caters specifically to your needs.) They're just a collection of fun, easy suggestions for you to make a nutritious lunch. My philosophy is that if you feed yourself normal, wholesome, healthy food on a regular basis, you have the best chance of being and staying healthy, and having plenty of energy to do your work and live your life.

I have designed these to be sturdy recipes. A little more of this and a little less of that will not make or break the end result: it's just lunch food, remember? If you see an ingredient you do not like, or are allergic to, just replace it with one you like. If you dislike celery, substitute a vegetable that is also crunchy such as carrots. Just look for a similar quality and I'm sure you'll come up with great combinations.

The only place you cannot do this is in the baking recipes. Every ingredient in those recipes has a specific function that cannot randomly be substituted. Wheat flour, for instance, can make gluten, which is what creates the sturdy matrix in bread. Substituting buckwheat flour would result in a completely different product.

Some of the recipes in this book also appear in my new cookbook, *The School Lunchbox Cookbook*. For this book I've made them a little more grown-up in taste, without including all sorts of weird ingredients or complicated procedures.

The concerns of this book are, happily, present-minded: What to eat for lunch today, tomorrow, this week? But we have our eye on the future as well. That's because one of the main inspirations behind *The Brown Bag Lunch Cookbook*, and its companion, *The School Lunchbox Cookbook*, was the unhappy fact that the problem of obesity is now global and not just American. It cuts across national lines. Germany, Greece (despite the highly touted Mediterranean diet), and Egypt, to cite just a few countries, all report obesity problems. It cuts across demographic categories, too, affecting young and old, rich and poor, men and women, boys and girls. Only Africa, North Korea, and some sections of the Asian subcontinent escape the obesity problem, but that is true, of course, because of severe food shortages and poverty in those areas.

However, as this book went to press, the ground was shifting under the feet of the giant food-producing corporations, worldwide. *The New York Times* reported in mid-2003 that "... the War Against Fat has become a global conflict, and the rules of engagement appear to be changing." The news—which all consumers should be watching—was that in the United States actual or threatened lawsuits against the food giants had pushed them to announce sweeping changes in the ways they make and market their products. On the European side, government regulators were threatening to require similar changes in the practices of the food giants, including foreign companies importing to the European market. Kraft Foods, one of the biggest U.S. food producers and exporters, announced it would reduce portion sizes, reduce the amount of trans fats in many products, reduce sugar and salt, and would stop marketing directly to children in the schools.

Of course all of these announced changes were to come about gradually over several years, and some were still in the research phase because corporations like Kraft (Nestle, Unilever, Groupe Danone) also have to satisfy their stockholders' demands for continued profits. It would take a real leap of faith to believe that Kraft, controlled by a holding company that also owns the tobacco giant Philip Morris, will make good on all these promises, that it isn't just buying time, or placating the critics. But if these companies and other fast-food chains like McDonald's, which had also announced substantial changes to come, follow through, there could be a beneficial impact on consumers' eating habits. Only, however, if consumers also discipline themselves, and that brings us back to the gist of this cookbook. We say: Don't count on the food giants and the fast-food folks to help you solve your lunchtime menu needs. Read this book, use it often, share the recipes, and have fun while you, yourself, take charge of the sugars, salts, fats, and calories in your lunchtime diet.

Introduction

If you are ready to cook, go right ahead. But if you are looking for some suggestions, tips, or inspiration, here they are.

Life in the Fast Lane

Life in North America has changed radically in the last hundred years, and it has changed at breakneck speed in the last forty or so years. But our bodies and genetics do not change as quickly, and the rules by which our bodies organize themselves are the same now as they were 3,000 years ago. Our needs for sleep, movement, clean water, wholesome food, unpolluted air, entertainment, and community have not changed, but our society *has* changed dramatically in the ways it provides for these needs.

No longer do we go to sleep when it is dark and wake up when it gets light again. Instead we can have bright lights around us all day and all night, and we use an alarm clock to wake us before we are done sleeping. Physical movement is no longer needed to attend to basic chores, such as hunting animals, tending the fields, chopping wood, or kneading bread. We now drive to work, buy our food already prepared, and sit all night, isolated in our own little house, watching our entertainment pour forth from little boxes called televisions and computer terminals.

Our water has a different pH level now than it did 3,000 years ago, our vegetables have foreign genes injected or designed into them, and we eat massive quantities of foods that nature did not produce. No wonder our bodies are in revolt! The assault on our bodies is so extensive that the damage is no longer waiting to reveal itself until middle or old age but is manifesting itself in our children.

I know that there is a lot of controversy about food, diet, and health. You will have no problem finding "authorities" who will argue long and loud that whatever they are doing to the food and water is not the problem. Some tell you fat is the problem. Others shout at you that we are poisoning ourselves with too much protein. "Experts" tell you that microwaving is completely safe; that an "enriched" product is the equivalent of, or superior to, the original natural product; that synthetic vitamins are of the same quality as the ones found in food; that the minute quantities of artificial color, artificial flavor, and preservatives added to food could not possibly matter; and that frozen foods have the same nutritional value as fresh.

There is no easy answer to this debate, no one single factor that's gone wrong. But the disaster created by the combination of all these factors is most visible in the fact that Americans are getting obese and sick at alarming rates.

If you really want to understand how fast food has changed the way Americans—and increasingly other peoples as well—eat and think about food, read *Fast Food Nation* by Eric Schlosser. Study Schlosser like you did your texts in school, and mark up his book with a highlighter, lest you forget the most important points. His analysis is worth your time.

And listen to the news. The fast-food companies and major food manufacturers are under siege. Some are being sued in class action suits modeled on the successful lawsuits brought against tobacco companies. While it's clear that some of the big guns are responding to the public outcry and are beginning to make some long overdue changes, we still have to be vigilant. For the foreseeable future, mass-produced processed food is unlikely to be geared toward our or our children's health.

Take a look at the nutritional information posted on the Web sites of some of your favorite fast-food places. I think you'll be surprised at what you find. The difference between a small order of french fries and a supersize one (according to the McDonald's Web site) is an increase of 400 calories. Look at its Caesar salad and you'll find that the salad (without chicken) is a very reasonable 90 calories, but when you choose Creamy Caesar Dressing to top it, you add an additional 190 calories. (A word of warning: Commercial salad dressing in individual packages, such as the ones you get at a supermarket, often contain more than one serving, but the calories are given to you per serving. Pretty tricky, right?) Burger King chooses to give you the calories of its sandwiches with and without the mayo; that's a 160 calorie difference right there. And two of their chocolate chip cookies add up to a whopping 440 calories; are they really worth it?

Some single foods are also terribly high in calories by themselves. A vanilla thirty-two-ounce shake is 1140 calories! Size matters, make no mistake: A twelve-ounce soft drink (child size) has about 110 calories, but the forty-two-ounce contains 410 calories.

And then there's sodium. Americans get most of their sodium intake from processed foods. Almost every meal out will give you a large dose. If you are sensitive to sodium, you already know that you will hold water in your hands and feet after a meal out. High blood pressure can usually be taken down a notch or two by limiting sodium (even a modest decline has major health benefits). The tastiest way to do that is to make your own lunches and season them in all the other ways the recipes suggest.

Eating Out: The Problem

Not so very long ago, eating out was considered a treat. It was a way to celebrate a special occasion, and the calorie, fat content, or nutritional content of the meal was not relevant to most people. Times clearly have changed.

Even if you use this book to help you make your own lunch, you will still be going out some. Here are some eating-out tips to help you eat wisely.

Commercial pizzas usually drip with cheese. One of the easiest ways to cut calories is to ask for half the cheese on the pizza. Since pizzas are all individually made, it is easy enough for a shop to put on less. Ask for lots of vegetables and no meats, and you'll be doing a lot better than the standard pepperoni version.

Many of the most popular sandwich shops offer information on the fat content of their sandwiches, so you can make an enlightened choice. Turkey breast and lean roast beef sandwiches can be good nutritional bargains, especially if you hold the mayo and load up on fresh veggies.

However, corned beef sandwiches (naturally high in fat and sodium), egg salad and tuna fish salad (with high-fat mayonnaise), turkey clubs (with lots of bacon), and grilled cheese (loads of fat in the cheese and in the grilling) pack in the calories. Watch out for the vegetarian sandwich, too; the cheese and mayonnaise dressing add a lot of calories to an otherwise virtuous choice. Your best bet is to ask for extra veggies, skip the mayo, get a side salad, use only a little dressing, and don't even think about chips.

The drill at other restaurants is pretty much the same for all cuisines: If it is deep-fried (calamari, nachos, cheese fries, deep-fried onion), contains loads of fat (Spanakopita, fried mozzarella sticks), has loads of cheese (pasta Alfredo, sour cream on Mexican food), or features huge quantities of high-fat meats, your arteries will shudder at what you are giving them to handle.

Go with dishes that have loads of vegetables (Buddha's delight), order grilled and steamed lean fish and chicken, and get healthy side dishes (plain salad or salsa instead of sour cream and guacamole).

Beware of the hidden calories in the little sides that look like they might not matter, a handful of peanuts, and a few slices of garlic bread. They will really add up quickly. No matter what the food shop, do NOT "oversize," "double stuff," or in any other way "pile it on." Calorie counts that might otherwise be within tolerable limits will go off the charts that way.

Oh, and in case you didn't know: The french fries you pick off your friend's plate and the few spoonfuls of her ice cream sundae DO have calories and will count!

Planning: What We Can Learn from Take-out Food

There is one thing to learn from fast-food restaurants. Why do you think a McDonald's or Kentucky Fried Chicken restaurant can serve you a meal as quickly as they can? Do you think they first put up the water to boil potatoes once you order it? Do you think they start washing the lettuce when you first order a salad? Of course not! In the food business, as in every business, preparation is the mark of a professional. Planning and cooking ahead will make a huge difference, not only in the nutrition you and your family receive, but also in your budget and your peace of mind.

Once a week make a schedule for lunch meals, and make a shopping list at the same time. See what treats are still in the freezer, and plan to make one more batch of muffins to keep your supply replenished. Make sure you have the ingredients for items to be prepared well in advance, or else put them on the shopping list.

Make a similar plan for your breakfasts and dinners, which again will give you a great measure of control and peace of mind. Instead of take-out burgers on the days when nobody is home at the same time and everybody is eating on the run, plan to make a large pot of soup, which can be kept warm in a Crock-Pot, and a large chef salad. Sunday supper with the family—such as a roast surrounded with root vegetables—can be a simple dish that can be in the oven a long time, rather than a last-minute decision for a delivered pizza. Making a large batch of pasta one night gives you leftovers for pasta vegetable salad two days later. Placing stew ingredients in your Crock-Pot the night before, and starting it in the morning, means that you come home to a warm meal ready to eat the moment you step in the door. And, ah, the aroma!

Making this sort of plan also means a huge savings: Take-out food is never as cheap as a homemade meal. At the back end, you'll be saving money, too, because your healthier family will spend less on cold remedies and doctors' bills.

The Foods We Need

I can think of no other field where so many experts disagree so loudly with each other about such vital information. People who have degrees in biochemistry, nutrition, and medicine hotly debate our most basic nutritional questions. Are carbohydrates good for us or not? What kind of fats do we need and how much? We need five or seven or ten fruits or vegetables, but which kinds? Do ketchup and applesauce really count toward our daily quota of fruits and vegetables?

There is no way that I can answer these questions for you. This book's collection of recipes is designed to give you a good variety of all sorts of nutrients, with special emphasis on recipes with fruits and vegetables, because that is where many of us fall short. If you are struggling with weight issues, you know you need to go easy on the high-calorie foods such as baked goods, high-fat cheeses, oils, nuts, and high-fat meats, and increase your intake of fresh fruit and vegetables. I think you'll find plenty of options in the recipes in this book.

Of course you need to follow your health provider's specific advice about the following comments if your health is at stake.

We Need Fat

Fat was the "bad" food for a long time, but now, with the resurgence in popularity of the Atkins diet, fat is a "good" food. Either way, having some fat in your diet is absolutely essential for everything from beautiful skin and hair to well-functioning nerves and reproductive systems.

What I have done in these recipes is to emphasize olive oil, since nearly everybody seems to agree that it is a healthy fat. I use butter instead of margarine, because I believe that it is safer to have a little saturated fat than a lot of the chemicals that are in margarine. Avocados are high in calories, for a vegetable, but they do have excellent-quality fat and the most vitamin E of any vegetable.

We Need Protein

Proteins are the building blocks of the body, providing growth and repair in countless different ways. An adequate supply is necessary for normal growth, for the formation of hormones, for the process of blood clotting, and for thousands of other processes. Protein does not raise the blood sugar levels the way refined carbohydrates do and therefore does not spike your energy with the inevitable drop later.

Are you one of the many people who are becoming vegetarians? If this is a short-term experiment, you don't need to do much. But if you are serious about vegetarianism, make sure you know how to balance out your intake of food to get adequate protein. Get a respected book on vegetarianism to get the right information, especially the need for absorbable vitamin B_{12} and getting adequate and balanced amino acids.

Protein options for lunch include shaved meats such as roast beef and ham; poultry such as chicken and turkey; hard-boiled eggs; cheese, sliced or cubed or string cheese; yogurt (with live cultures); cottage cheese; nut butters such as peanut or cashew; hummus or bean dips; or stews or soups with meats and beans. If you like and tolerate dairy products, milk is a source of protein and much needed calcium.

We Need Carbohydrates

Carbohydrates are necessary for energy and fiber and the many vitamins and minerals they contain.

However, not all carbohydrates are equal. By the time the food industry does its magic with our grains, fruits, and vegetables, these foods are totally transformed. It is true, for instance, that sugar is a carbohydrate, but it will not give you the nutrients the way an apple, which has lots of sugar, will. Good, dense carbohydrates are whole wheat bread, whole wheat pita bread, whole wheat bagels, whole wheat tortillas, sweet potatoes, brown rice, beans, and whole wheat pasta. All fruits and vegetables contain primarily carbohydrates and are absolutely essential to supply necessary vitamins, minerals,

and other food factors as well. No pill, however splendid the multivit-
amin might be, can ever replace the perfect balance of nutrients
Mother Nature placed in fruits and vegetables. For a good list of
vegetables and fruits, look at the introductions to the salad and fruit
chapters.

What you do not need is white sugar, white rice, and white flour.
Though these substances start out as foods, they are stripped of
every conceivable useful nutrient by the commercial food industry. In
"enriched" white flour, some few (cheaply and synthetically made)
vitamins have been added back in to compensate for the nutrients
that have been leached and bleached out. There is probably no more
significant change that you can make to improve your health than to
cut out refined sugars in all forms. The main, hidden way that refined
sugars are making their way into our diet right now is through the
addition of corn syrup to a stunning array of foods, from soda to
tomato ketchup. Read food labels carefully, look up the ingredients
you don't understand, and don't be a passive, misled consumer.

We Need Vitamins, Minerals, and Antioxidants

It seems that every month scientists "discover" a new something that
we ought to eat to keep us healthy. You sometimes wonder how all
the previous generations ever got by!

There is a much easier way to keep track of all the stuff your
body needs: Eat colorful foods and limit white and beige foods. In
What Color Is Your Diet? (HarperCollins, 2002), Dr. David Heber
explains that different groups of fruits and vegetables have different
plant chemicals in them that will protect your body in different ways.
I highly recommend his informative book, and in the introduction to
the salad chapter I give a few of Dr. Heber's tips and examples.

We Need Water

Water—plain old water—is what we need. Soda is never necessary
and should be a treat, not a normal part of your diet; it's got empty
calories that add unnecessary chemicals to your metabolism. If you

drink juice, look at the label to see that it is pure juice and not a sugary drink with a little bit of added token juice. Be aware that juice is very high in calories, and you might want to trade in a cup of apple juice for a cup of water and an apple. They're much healthier and much more filling.

Staples for the Pantry, Fridge, and Freezer

Keep these staples in your pantry, refrigerator, and freezer, and making a healthy meal—breakfast, lunch, and dinner—will be a snap.

Baking Powder

When the recipes in this book instruct you to "add baking powder," you are always best off sifting it first to make sure there are no clumps. Finding a clump of baking powder in a muffin is a disgusting experience! When buying baking powder, be sure to get one with no aluminum additives, since this metal, even in trace amounts, is implicated in Alzheimer's disease.

Baking Soda

Finding a clump of baking soda in your quick bread is just as bad as baking powder, so be sure to sift it, too, before adding it.

Baking soda is activated by a "sour" or acid ingredient in the batter—either buttermilk or vinegar. The rising action (which is actually the making of small bubbles) is an immediate, chemical one and starts the moment the two ingredients find each other. If you mix a batter with baking soda too vigorously, you will break the bubbles, and your baked product will be flat. When you see baking soda in a recipe, it means that you will need to mix the batter with long efficient strokes, quickly but thoroughly, and not let the mixed batter sit. Pour the batter into the baking pan carefully as soon as it is mixed and bake it right away.

Beans and Pulses

Filled with protein, calcium, iron, and zinc, beans and pulses (the dried, edible seeds of legumes, such as lentils and peas) deserve a starring place in your kitchen.

After a night of presoaking, dried beans can be cooked quickly (just throw away the soaking water to lose some of the gas-inducing chemicals). Using canned beans is a great shortcut, especially if you use products that do not have added chemicals. Having cans of chickpeas, black beans, red kidney beans, and white beans in your pantry means that soups, salads, and spreads are just minutes away.

Lentils and split peas do not need presoaking and can be cooked in stews and soups until they are softened.

Butter

In my recipes I use sweet (unsalted) butter for a very simple reason: I love the taste of butter, and I distrust margarine. Use your common sense here and read the ingredients on the margarine package. Your body is not meant to ingest chemicals; it was designed to digest food! Margarine was invented as a cheap, durable butter substitute for the soldiers in Napoleon's army. If you are under strict doctor's orders not to eat butter, then follow the doctor's advice. Otherwise, use butter with moderation and enjoy every little bit of it.

Buttermilk Powder

I like baked goods made with buttermilk—the liquid left over after the cream has been skimmed from the whole milk. I seldom needed a full quart of it when cooking, though, so I would resist making recipes calling for buttermilk, because I didn't want the rest to go to waste. Dry buttermilk powder is a great solution. It is easy to reconstitute and gives excellent results. If you'd rather use fresh buttermilk in any of my recipes, just substitute the water part in the recipes (which is meant to reconstitute the powder) with fresh buttermilk.

Eggs

For just a little bit more money, you can get organic eggs in many supermarkets, and certainly in health food stores. These come from chickens that are fed a healthy diet, not one filled with hormones and other chemicals that can find their way into the egg. The little extra expense would seem more than worth it. When you crack a natural egg, you will notice that the yolk is nice and high and probably very yellow, and the taste is much better, too.

Fish

Fish is a great source of protein and tuna fish is a great lunchtime favorite. Oily fish such as salmon and sardines give us good doses of omega-3 fatty acids, which are necessary for healthy skin and good heart function. Canned sardines still have their bones in, which you can eat; this will give you a great boost of calcium.

Flour

In most of my baking recipes, I use whole wheat flour. White flour, called all-purpose flour, is made by eliminating the very ingredients that make flour good for us: vitamins, minerals, fiber, and all manner of micronutrients. Replacing a few of those nutrients with some chemically produced vitamins cannot compare to the real thing. When I do use white flour, I make sure that it is not bleached.

Refrigerate your flour, since the fats in it can go rancid, and try to buy it from a store that has a lot of turnover so that it is as fresh as possible.

Fruits

Look in the beginning of the chapter on fruit for a full discussion of some of their benefits. Having a selection of fresh and dried fruit on hand is a good way to make sure you include variety, nutrition, and deliciousness in your meals.

Herbs

Fresh and dried herbs add flavor and flair to any dish. Grow some on a windowsill or in a corner in your garden so you can pluck some fresh when you like. Parsley, basil, dill, mint, rosemary, oregano, and thyme will give you a good beginning selection and will allow you to flavor many dishes. If you like specific herb combinations, make them up in half-cup quantities. To flavor vinaigrettes I have handy a jar of salad herbs, which consists of oregano, thyme, basil, and a little dill.

Meat and Poultry

For many people meat and poultry are the main source of protein, so it is important that they are of high quality. Choose lean varieties of meat and take the skin off chicken, where most of the fat resides. For your lunch choose low-fat varieties of lunchmeat and avoid highly processed meats, to limit your intake of preservatives and such. Lunch is a perfect way to use up little bits of leftover dinner, so toss some leftover chicken or little bits of last night's roast into a salad.

Milk

Throughout these recipes I have used 2 percent milk. Feel free to use whole milk or nonfat milk. The results will be slightly different, but none of these recipes is so sensitive that it will significantly affect the result.

Mushrooms

Because of their distinctive taste and texture, a few mushrooms added to a dish instantly make the food more interesting. In the last few years, many more varieties of mushrooms are finding their way to the supermarket shelves, so experiment to see what you like. Canned mushrooms have almost no flavor, so go with fresh if you can.

Nuts

Nuts are loaded with protein as well as fat, so use them to spice up your meals—but use them in moderation. A few Brazil nuts supply a hefty dose of selenium, necessary for male fertility. Almonds are high in vitamin E, as are hazelnuts and peanuts, and almonds have a moderate ability to help lower blood cholesterol. Chestnuts are not fatty but are mostly carbohydrates, and are a great wintertime snack.

Pistachio nuts have some iron in them, pecans are full of zinc, and walnuts contain linoleic acid (which is thought to lower cholesterol). Keep a supply of these nuts on hand and enjoy them for their varied tastes and health benefits.

Store all nuts in the refrigerator—or even the freezer—because the fat in the nuts can and does go rancid when stored an extended time at room temperature. For that same reason, buy your nuts from a health food store that stores its nuts in the refrigerator and has a brisk turnover.

Oats

Keep rolled oats on hand and you can always have a fast, nutritious bowl of oatmeal for breakfast. Oats are also a key ingredient in various baked goods. Oats are rich in iron and zinc and seem to be able to help lower the cholesterol levels in the blood. Oat bran, which is rich in fiber, can be added to dishes such as meatloaf.

Olive Oil

For dressings and sautéing I use extra-virgin olive oil, because I like the fruity taste and because it is "heart healthy." For baking I use extra-light-tasting olive oil, because I don't want the taste of olives in my muffins and cakes.

Onions and Their Relatives

Onions, chives, leeks, and garlic all belong to the same botanical family. I love them all and find it difficult to cook without them. However, in this cookbook I have used them sparingly, because it is sometimes hard to get rid of their smell on one's breath. Actually, garlic is not just smelled on the breath; even your sweat will smell of garlic if you eat enough of it. If I have to talk face to face to people, or work in a confined space, using these vegetables in lunch dishes can sometimes be a problem. My experience, however, is that once onions or leeks are cooked, they become tamer and the smell is gone after I brush my teeth.

Rice

Rice has been a staple food in China and most of India for many thousands of years. Brown rice takes a lot longer to cook, but it is so much healthier for you than white rice that it is worth every minute. Keep fully cooked rice in the freezer (packed in baggies with the air squeezed out) for a quick meal or rice salad. Brown rice is a good source of B vitamins and fiber.

Basmati rice is aromatic and perfect for exotic dishes, such as Indian curries, as well as rice pudding.

Spices

Spices, like herbs, boost the flavor and the appeal of food. Ground cinnamon, cloves, nutmeg, ginger, cumin, cayenne pepper, and turmeric are a good variety to choose from. If you like certain combinations, mix up a few tablespoons and keep them in an airtight jar. I keep a mix of cinnamon, cloves, a little nutmeg, and a little mace on hand to flavor cakes, since I love that combination.

Sugar and Other Sweets

Light brown sugar is the sugar I use most often in baking, mainly because I find it has more flavor than white sugar. Dark brown sugar has a distinctive molasses taste, which is too overpowering in most baked goods, except gingerbread. I love working with maple syrup and honey, but a little goes a long way, so don't use too generous a hand.

If you have a strong reaction to sugar or are diabetic, you'll have to find other cookbooks to help with suggestions. I have found that "naturally sweet" baking books end up using honey liberally, and that will most likely affect you in the same way sugar does. Your best bet would be cookbooks geared specifically toward diabetics, who have to avoid the adrenaline spike caused by the sugar. For all of us, the best way to handle high-sugar snacks is by making sure we have protein in the same meal and to make sure the portion is governed by common sense and not by desire.

Tahini

Tahini, a paste made from ground sesame seeds, has been used as a food since at least 3000 B.C. It continues to be a delicious and healthful addition to our pantry. It is an essential ingredient in hummus and it is very high in calcium, the great natural relaxer of muscles and minds.

Vegetables and Salad Greens

Please refer to the beginning of the salad chapter for a list of vegetable suitable for salads and garnishes for lunches. Needless to say, these are pivotal in good nutrition and healthy bodies.

Vinegar

When I need to use vinegar, I mainly use apple cider vinegar, and often one with a live culture in it (vinegar is made in the same way that yogurt, cheese, and wine are, by letting microorganisms act on a food). There is a lot of literature around that suggests that apple cider vinegar is healthful, and that is why I stick with it. Besides, I happen to like its flavor. I am sure a person in your local health food store could tell you a lot more about it. I use balsamic vinegar in my dressings a lot, because its sweet taste is so wonderful. Rice vinegar is not nearly as acidic as most vinegars; it works best when I want just a hint of tart.

There are many flavored vinegars on the market that will give you a lot of variety when you are making your own salad dressings, but I have limited my selection in this book so that you can easily make these recipes with a minimum of new ingredients.

Yogurt

Yogurt is made when certain bacteria interact with milk—bacteria that are very beneficial for our intestinal health. If yogurts have "live cultures," these bacteria are still active; when you eat the yogurt, they will be useful to you. If they do not, then you are just eating a soured-milk product with no additional health benefit.

The fat content of the yogurt you use will depend on your personal preference. I prefer the taste of full-fat and low-fat yogurts, but nonfat yogurt does save fat calories and works perfectly well in certain recipes.

If you use relatively little of it, then full-fat or low-fat will be just fine. If you are concerned about your milkfat intake, use low-fat or nonfat. Experiment and see what works best for you.

Tools for Easy Lunches

Not everyone loves cooking. So for those who feel a bit out of their depth in the kitchen, here are some notes about kitchen tools—all meant to make lunch prep time, and all your other cooking time, more convenient and simple.

The less you like to cook, the simpler you might want to make your kitchen environment. Eliminate clutter and confusion and make sure that the kitchen tools you get are of a top quality and that they please you. High-quality tools are often a little more expensive, but they will generally perform better and with less hassle than the cheapo stuff, so you'll eliminate some frustration.

Baking Cups

These are paper or foil cups that line muffin tins. Baking cups just about totally eliminate the scraping and cleaning up of a muffin pan, a job I totally detest. If you use paper cups and eat the muffins while they are still warm, a lot of the muffin will stick to the paper. However, once the muffins cool, the paper will peel off nicely. Foil baking cups do not stick to the muffin, even while warm. If you like to serve muffins hot, this is the way to go, or consider investing in a high-quality nonstick muffin tin.

You can also spray the muffin tin with a nonstick spray. If you spray it thoroughly, your muffins will come out easily, but you will have to wash the tin after cooking a batch.

Baking Utensils

Nonstick baking sheets are worth their weight in gold since they will save you lots of annoying scrubbing time. Use only plastic utensils on these and all other nonstick surfaces, no matter what the label says. If you bake cookies a lot, get a roll of parchment paper; this is how restaurants save on scraping and washing cookie sheets.

Two round pans, one 9-by-9-inch pan, one 9-by-13-inch pan, and a pie plate will be plenty to start with if baking is not really your bag. Add a decent set of measuring spoons and cups and a few mixing bowls and you can do almost everything in this book. There are loads more utensils you could get if you decide baking is your forte.

Blender

There are things a food processor won't do but a blender will. For example, the blender is ideal for making fruit shakes and salad dressings. I like to keep frozen bananas in the freezer to mix with orange juice, and possibly some unsweetened yogurt, to make a wonderful, refreshing snack.

Containers, Baggies, and Such

When you start taking lunch with you to work, you will find that you will, inevitably, lose some containers. My advice is to get usable, but not very expensive stuff, so you won't feel tense about them. Have handy a large supply of baggies in various sizes, plastic wrap, lots of containers, and a thermos or two so that you can easily transport your lunch. A few little containers, half-filled with water in the freezer, will give you instant cold packs when you need them.

Food Processor

I use my food processor all the time, and I cannot recommend it highly enough. I have an old one, which has stood up to unbelievable use and abuse, and I consider it the one essential electrical tool in my kitchen. Every other thing I can fake—I can toast bread in a frying pan, I can open a can without electricity, I could just possibly live without my blender (though that is appliance #2), but there are a lot of dishes I would not make without my trusty food processor. It is worth learning how to use the various attachments so you can shred carrots, mix cookie dough, and whip cream with ease and confidence. If you cook a lot, a second bowl is a worthwhile investment.

Pots and Pans

You don't need many, but try to get good pots and pans. Please throw out aluminum ones; who knows if the leached aluminum actually has a connection to Alzheimer's, but why take the risk? Minimally you need a large stockpot for making stocks, a frying pan (preferably with a high-quality nonstick coating), and two pots with lids. For steaming veggies, a steamer, which you can insert in the large pot or one of the pans, is great.

Buy all of your pans either with an enamel coating, or—my personal favorite—high-grade stainless steel clad copper. The latter heat very evenly and will not hold a flavor or aroma. As you start cooking more, you might want a larger selection of pots and pans.

Spoons, Ladles, Whisks, Spatulas, and Such

Unless you just love to cook, you don't need as much as you think. There are so many neat gadgets around, you could easily accumulate bushels full of them. This only makes most reluctant cooks more confused and frustrated. Streamline your kitchen by placing in a box all the gadgets you have not used in two years. Date the box and forget about it for six months. If you can't remember what was in it and you haven't missed anything, it is time for you to have a tag sale! In the meantime you will have gained drawers that are not too full and are easier to keep clean.

If you love to cook, seeing the zester, an egg slicer, a strawberry huller, a cherry pitter, and a green bean slicer in your drawer will probably inspire you. Even then I suggest that you keep the specialty stuff separate, so that you can more easily grab the everyday stuff. A long-handled spoon or two (made from wood or stainless steel), a whisk, a rubber spatula or two (one large, one small) and a flat spatula are what you need close to the stove.

Other than your ordinary cutlery, you need a few good, sharp knives—a small one to peel things, a medium one to chop, and a long skinny one to slice bread. Look to see what you actually use. I cook with a lot of lemon juice and have two juicers; I almost always grate things in the food processor so I rarely use the hand grater; and I love my vegetable peeler.

The bottom line is, the less you like to cook, the simpler you should make your kitchen, so you don't become overwhelmed.

Keeping Lunch Safe

Obviously it is critical that the lunch you pack is safe to eat! Keep these common sense precautions in mind.

Food "spoils" because food-borne pathogens, aka germs, grow on food surfaces in great numbers. The two keys to preventing this condition are: Keep the food as clean as possible to begin with and then give the germs the least friendly environment in which to multiply.

Scrub all fruits and vegetables; just because they look clean coming into the house from the supermarket does not mean they are fit to eat.

Really clean the containers you use to pack a lunch. If you use a lunchbox, wipe the interior once a week with a paper towel dipped in a very dilute bleach solution (1 teaspoon in a gallon of water).

Pathogens grow most slowly in very cold or very hot environments, so the goal is to have cold foods cold and hot foods hot until they are eaten. This precaution starts in the kitchen: Place food back in the refrigerator as soon as it is practical after lunch preparations. If you are making a chicken salad from chicken left over from dinner, do that before you do the dishes, so that the chicken salad can get cold right away.

Frozen juice boxes are a great way to keep a lunch cold in a lunchbox (by lunchtime, the drink will defrost). So are ice packs, of course, as well as recycled, well-cleaned, small water bottles. At night fill small water bottles half full with water or a beverage, place the cap on loosely so some air can escape, and freeze them. In the morning fill them up the rest of the way. (A fully frozen bottle might not be sufficiently defrosted in the few hours between packing the food and lunchtime.) Be sure to place the cap on securely before you pack the bottle in the lunch bag.

Consider buying an insulated lunchbox to keep lunch cold—or hotter—longer, the same way you might take a cooler with you in the trunk of your car when you buy frozen foods on a hot day.

For cold foods, pre-chill a thermos bottle by filling it with cold water and ice cubes for five minutes. Pour out the water and refill with the cold food.

Rinse a thermos with boiling water before you fill it with hot stew or soup; that way it will really stay warm. Never fill the bottle all the way to the top. Leave about an inch of headroom to provide space for the top (on good thermos bottles, tops screw in like corks).

Do not use a thermos to transport carbonated beverages: The top could come off with quite a bang after being shaken all morning in a lunch bag.

Hints and Tips

Remember Your Favorites

Keep a list of foods you decide are yummy and healthy. Too many times I have "forgotten" a good recipe that I really liked. If you need visual reminders, a special notebook, blackboard, or bulletin board are good ways of keeping track of recipes and copies of recipes. Make lists in the five basic categories: sandwiches, fruits and veggies, snacks, desserts, and drinks. You can paste in recipes you cut from magazines and newspapers. Use this list to inspire you as you make a weekly plan.

Slow Down

The idea that eating is an experience that we have to do as quickly as possible is bizarre to me. Speed is admirable when it is connected with concepts such as doing taxes, tooth extraction, or waiting in line at the supermarket checkout. But eating is neither painful nor boring; it is a joyful, sensual, healing, nourishing, social experience. So why is speed so essential? If you are wolfing down meals, trying to fit them in your schedule, and not sitting down, maybe you need to look at your priorities.

Taking time to sit down and enjoy your meal will help you to digest it properly and to stop before overstuffing yourself, by giving your brain time to register that your belly is full.

Eat Breakfast

I know families who get up half an hour earlier than they did before, just so that they can all sit down in the morning and have a simple breakfast together. This does not necessarily mean a lot of extra work. Cooking oatmeal in a slow-cooker overnight assures an automatic warm bowl in the morning. The bread maker you were so enthusiastic about a few years ago could be dusted off and a fresh loaf of bread could be waiting for you when you wake up. A child can be in charge of setting the breakfast table in the evening, after supper, so that it is ready for you in the morning. Eggs can be cracked the night before and sitting in the blender bowl in the refrigerator waiting to be whipped and made into a quick omelet. Add a little chopped, leftover spinach salad from the night before and you have a gourmet meal as fast as it takes for you to wait at the fast-food drive-up window.

There are plenty of ideas in this book that could double for breakfast, and I highly recommend you do that. It helps you to feel more alert in the morning and helps with hunger management throughout the day. On top of that, a study described in the *FDA Consumer* magazine in 2002 showed that 95 percent of the people who succeeded in losing thirty pounds or more ate breakfast more than four times a week.

Eating Breakfast on the Run

For those mornings when breakfast just does not work out, be sure to grab something to eat on the run. You might want to make little snack bags ahead of time with cereal, dried fruit, and some nuts (see the Gorp recipe in the Between Breakfast and Lunch chapter), easy things you and your family can eat on the run. Homemade (healthy!) muffins with a piece of cheese are also great to grab and eat. Grab an extra small juice, milk box, or water bottle to wet your whistle, so that you are not just drinking coffee.

Bag Your Own

The healthier chips, such as vegetable chips, usually don't come in convenient single-serving sizes, or they are packaged two servings per bag. Let me ask you: Have you ever eaten just half a bag of chips, pretzels, or cookies? So beat the system: Portion them out into small, resealable bags yourself. You can also do this with other snacks, such as yogurt-covered almonds and pretzels, that you can buy in bulk at health food stores.

No Soggy Sandwiches

Packing certain items separately might be a good idea. Sometimes a sandwich becomes soggy if it is packed the night before or even in the morning, so you might be tempted to not eat it when you get to lunch. You can avoid some of the "soggy" issue by placing a lettuce leaf between the filling and the bread.

A Ketchup Saved

The next time you order take-out food, save the extra packages of salt, pepper, ketchup, mustard, and soy sauce. They're great to pack in a lunch.

Bundle Your Utensils

Here's a perfect little job while you are watching your favorite television show. Wrap plastic forks, spoons, and knives in paper napkins

Yes, you can freeze sandwiches ahead of time, but you cannot freeze all sandwich fillings successfully. I would not freeze sandwiches for more than one or two months. Experiment with some sandwiches and take them to work, so that you can be sure the taste and texture will work out to your own satisfaction before you make them in bulk.

Snacks, such as muffins, can also be frozen.

Freeze unsweetened applesauce in small, tightly closing containers. In the morning you can pack them with your lunch, and they will keep it nice and cold. By lunchtime, the applesauce will be mostly defrosted.

What you cannot freeze:
Eggs (as in egg salad)
Fresh fruits, with a few exceptions (see the Fruits chapter)
Greens (lettuce, celery, etc.)
Mayonnaise
Potatoes
Tomatoes
Yogurt

Some of the things you can freeze:
All breads, bagels and rolls (slice bagels and rolls first)
Cream cheese
Hard cheeses (cheddar, Swiss, etc.)
Hummus
Jelly and jam
Ketchup
Muffins
Mustard
Peanut and other nut butters
Pickle relish
Sliced meats, chicken, turkey, etc.

before you need them. Close the napkin bundle with a rubber band and place them in a basket, ready for a month's worth of lunches. Take a few bundles to work to keep in your desk.

Send a Little Kiss

As corny as it is, a Hershey's "kiss" does carry a special little message along with its little burst of chocolate. So if you are making lunch for a special sweetie, you can include one for a special message. And hey, if you are making your own lunch, pack a kiss for yourself and leave the lunchroom wondering!

Variety Is Fun

Buy napkins, paper plates, and utensils in fun, colorful designs to add a burst of design and color to your lunch.

Pool Together

If you work in an office, you might consider making a lunch-pool. Find four like-minded friends and make up a schedule. Be sure that you all agree on the foods that you'd like to eat (so that offending ingredients do not show up and that the calories are within tolerable limits for everybody), and who cooks on what day. Now all you have to do is make lunch for five on one day per week and the other four lunches will be cooked by your friends.

Potluck Lunch

Every so often, have a potluck lunch at your office. You could work around a specific theme—say, all Italian foods—or just sign up to bring in something you like to make. This will make lunch considerably more interesting and you're sure to find some good recipes you want to try out at home.

Polly Wants a Cracker?

Crackers are great to eat with soup or salad, but be careful about what you buy. Read the package: Does it have whole wheat or whole rye flour? Or is it filled with white flour, sugar, corn syrup, and all sorts of chemicals only a scientist can pronounce? Stick with high fiber, whole wheat, whole rye, spelt, or other natural crackers to get the most oomph from your lunch.

Clean Your Plate

If you find portion control an issue, and most of us do, try putting all your food on a plate before you start to eat. There is something reassuring about a full plate; it makes you think you'll be full. And use a small plate, rather than one of those huge platters. Cover at least half of your plate with a bright green salad; watch out for the calories in dressings, and you are on your way to getting a balanced lunch.

Eat Your Fruit; Don't Just Drink It

Fruit juices, even the "unsweetened" ones, are very high in calories, from 112 to 154 calories per cup, while most medium-size fruits have only 60 to 80 calories. Think about it: one cup of apple juice, or an apple plus a handful of strawberries and a glass of water?

In addition, the fiber in fruit will keep you feeling full longer.

Teas for Health

Green tea and rooibos (pronounced roy-boss) tea have been in the news because of the discovery of their anti-cancer properties. Make some tea at night, sweeten it with a little honey and lemon, and refrigerate it. This way you have a healthy drink to take with you in the morning.

Grilling Safety

If you live in a warm climate and grill frequently, you can easily prepare some great foods to take with you for the next day's lunch. Grilled chicken breast, grilled slices of steak, grilled vegetables are all great additions to a good lunch. There are several ways to make your fare healthier and reduce the cancer-causing substances that grilling causes.

Soaking your meats in marinades that have a vinegar or lemon base can add flavor and reduce harmful HCAs (heterocyclic amines) by more than 90 percent.

Spice your burgers with ground purple plums, grapes, berries, or tart cherries (a cup of fruit to a pound of ground beef) for a 90 percent reduction of HCAs. The addition of garlic, sage, and rosemary to beef or to marinades for chicken and the like also protects your health.

Read and Measure

At my local supermarket, I picked up a handy nutrition booklet with great information on the calories, fat, and sodium in the deli items. When you look at the numbers, it doesn't look so bad. But make no mistake: The chart gives the information for two ounces of meat and cheese, which is much less than your generous hand is likely to put on your own sandwich. If you want to watch your calories, buy a small kitchen scale and separate out two-ounce portions with deli paper, the same technique used by your favorite sandwich shop.

Stock Up at the Office

How annoying; you made a great salad for yourself, but you forgot to pack a fork! To avoid the hassle, make a little "lunch supply" corner in one of your desk drawers. Place the following in a plastic container: plastic utensils, sharp knife, napkin, can opener, and a rubber disc to help open a stubborn jar.

For the days when you forget your lunch at home or need a healthy snack, you might also like to keep on hand a few shelf-stable foods—instant soups, packs of crackers, peanut butter, rice cakes, air-popped popcorn, protein bars, juice boxes, dried fruit, and nuts. If you keep some instant oatmeal packages at your office and you have some milk in the refrigerator, you can make a quick breakfast if you had no time to eat at home.

Most offices have a refrigerator, with everybody sharing the space. Bringing in at the beginning of the week a cup of yogurt, some fruit, and a hard-boiled egg to keep handy assures you of a quick lunch.

Cook Ahead

Use your weekends to make large batches of food that you can easily take to work during the week. Having extra soup and muffins in the freezer and grilled chicken breasts, cut-up vegetables, and leftover rice and noodles in the refrigerator gives you the handy ingredients for making a quick lunch during the work week.

Get Outside and Move

Now that you don't have to wait in line to wait for lunch, you might have some time left over to go and take a walk. A walk around the block will help with digestion, get your blood flowing, and give you a boost of energy-giving oxygen.

People who suffer from SAD syndrome (Seasonal Affective Disorder) develop a depression that sets in during the winter when there is limited daylight. With the depression often comes overeating, especially of sugary foods. This points up the terrific importance of daylight; unless the weather is brutal, see if you can get some natural light on you.

Be Grateful

Maybe you can "adopt" a hungry child through one of the reputable child service agencies. Instead of buying nutritiously empty foods, you might decide to put some of that money toward helping to feed somebody who is really hungry.

Being grateful for the food you have, and sharing some with somebody who truly needs it, will fill an empty space in you no fast-food junk meal can possibly satisfy.

Between Breakfast and Lunch

ornings are often hectic times and a lot of us do not eat breakfast. In this chapter are some snacks you can take with you for a breakfast on the run, a midmorning snack, or as a dessert for your lunch.

Granola

This granola gets protein from the nuts, and iron from both the oats and the blackstrap molasses. It makes a delicious breakfast, or maybe you just want to have a little bag of it on hand when the munchies strike.

MAKES 2 QUARTS

4 cups rolled oats (not instant)
1 cup flaked, unsweetened
   coconut
½ cup oat bran
½ cup chopped almonds
½ cup chopped walnuts
½ cup pumpkin seeds
¼ cup sesame seeds
1 teaspoon ground cinnamon
½ teaspoon ground cloves
⅓ cup honey
⅓ cup extra-light-tasting
   olive oil
⅓ cup water
2 tablespoons blackstrap
   molasses
1 tablespoon almond extract
1 cup golden raisins

1. Preheat the oven to 350°F.

2. In a large bowl, combine the oats, coconut, oat bran, almonds, walnuts, pumpkin seeds, sesame seeds, cinnamon, and cloves. Mix well.

3. In a medium bowl, mix the honey, oil, water, molasses, and almond extract. Mix well.

4. Pour the honey mixture over the oat mixture. Spread the mixture in a large baking pan or two smaller baking pans. Bake for 20 minutes, stirring every 7 minutes. Watch out toward the end, because granola burns easily.

5. Let the granola cool. Stir in raisins. Store in closed tin.

Gorp Breakfast

Gorp is a mixture of dried fruits, nuts, and other little snacks that backpackers take along to give them concentrated energy. Who doesn't need an extra boost of energy at work? Gorp looks especially nice if the ingredients are roughly the same size. If you add a handful of cereal, you have a great take-along breakfast. Choose cereals that come in large pieces such as Chex, Cheerios, or miniature Shredded Wheat.

Your health food store is probably the best place to find fruit that is dried without sulfites or added sugar. It is also the best place to find nuts, which should always be refrigerated since the oil in them can go rancid quickly.

Dried fruit	Nuts	Crunch
Currants	Almonds	Crackers such as
Dried apples	Brazil nuts	fishies and oyster
Dried apricots	Cashews	crackers
Dried banana chips	Chestnuts	Popcorn (hot-air
Dried blueberries	Filberts	popped)
Dried cherries	Macadamia nuts	Pretzels
Dried coconut pieces	Peanuts	
Dried cranberries	Pecans	**Special treats**
Dried dates	Pine nuts	Animal crackers
Dried figs	Pistachios	Butterscotch chips
Dried mangoes	Pumpkin seeds	Carob chips
Dried papayas	Soy nuts	Cereal
Dried pineapples	Sunflower seeds,	Chocolate chips
Raisins	hulled	Chocolate-covered
	Walnuts	raisins or almonds
		M&Ms

Blueberry Bread

A very low-fat bread that makes a wonderful treat.

MAKES 1 LOAF

2 cups unbleached all-purpose flour

1½ teaspoons baking powder

½ teaspoon baking soda

½ teaspoon salt

1 egg

⅔ cup orange juice

½ cup maple syrup

3 tablespoons extra-light-tasting olive oil

1 cup blueberries

½ cup chopped walnuts

1. Preheat the oven to 350°F. Grease and flour a loaf pan.

2. In a large bowl mix the flour, baking powder, baking soda, and salt.

3. In a medium bowl beat the egg. Stir in the juice, syrup, and oil. Pour the juice mixture over the flour mixture. Add the blueberries and walnuts and mix in.

4. Bake the bread for 1 hour, or until a wooden toothpick inserted in the middle comes out clean. Let it cool in the pan for 10 minutes before unmolding. Let cool completely before slicing.

Cranberry Bread

When cranberries are in the supermarket in the fall, I buy a few extra packages to freeze so I can make cranberry bread and cranberry relish all year long. Though cranberries are much too tart to eat raw, in breads and muffins they give a nice tart bite. Cranberries also provide valuable nutrients, so be sure to eat them once in a while.

MAKES 1 LOAF

2 eggs
¾ cup light brown sugar
¼ cup unsalted butter, softened
½ cup orange juice
1 teaspoon vanilla extract
1 teaspoon orange extract
2 cups whole wheat flour
2 teaspoons baking powder
1 tablespoon dry buttermilk powder
1½ cups cranberries, frozen or fresh, washed and picked over

1. Preheat the oven to 375°F. Grease a loaf pan.

2. Put the eggs and sugar in a food processor fitted with the steel blade. Process until well blended. Add the butter, orange juice, and extracts. Process until well mixed. Add the flour, baking powder, and buttermilk powder and process until just mixed.

3. Place the batter in a large bowl, add the cranberries, and mix well. Pour the batter into the prepared pan. Bake for 50 minutes, or until a toothpick inserted into the middle comes out clean.

4. Let the bread cool in the pan for 10 minutes before unmolding. Let cool completely before slicing.

Banana Muffins

Muffins are easier to take to work than banana bread, so I adapted my bread recipe to create these muffins.

MAKES 9 MUFFINS

3 ripe bananas, cut in pieces
⅓ cup honey
¼ cup unsalted butter, cut in pieces
1 egg
1½ teaspoons vanilla extract
1½ cups whole wheat flour
2 teaspoons baking powder

1. Preheat the oven to 375°F. Spray a muffin pan with vegetable spray, or place 9 baking cups in the muffin pan.

2. Put the bananas, honey, butter, egg, and extract in a food processor fitted with the steel blade. Blend well. Add the flour and baking powder. Blend until mixed.

3. Spoon the batter into the muffin pan. Bake for 30 minutes or until a wooden toothpick inserted in the middle of a muffin comes out clean.

4. Let the muffins cool in the pan for 5 minutes. Remove from the pan and cool completely.

Carole's Muffins

There's nothing but healthy ingredients in these delicious muffins created by my friend Carole Owens. These are perfect for both breakfast and lunch, and they can be made very quickly!

MAKES 12 MUFFINS

2 cups rolled oats	1 egg
1 cup whole wheat flour	½ cup extra-light-tasting
¼ teaspoon salt	olive oil
½ teaspoon ground cinnamon	½ cup maple syrup
1 tablespoon baking powder	½ cup walnuts
⅓ cup water	½ cup raisins

1. Preheat the oven to 350°F. Spray a muffin pan with vegetable spray, or place baking cups in the muffin pan.

2. Pour the oats into a food processor fitted with the steel blade. With on/off pulses cut the oat flakes into small pieces. It is not necessary to grind the oats to flour.

3. Add the whole wheat flour, salt, cinnamon, and baking powder and mix. Add the water and the egg. Mix well. Add the oil and syrup and blend until well mixed. Add the walnuts and mix with little on/off pulses.

4. Add the raisins and mix lightly with a spoon (don't run the machine). With a spoon divide the batter among the muffin cups.

5. Bake for 20 minutes or until a wooden toothpick inserted in the middle of a muffin comes out clean. Let the muffins cool in the pan for a few minutes. Then remove from the pan and let cool completely.

VARIATION: Instead of raisins, try dried cranberries, cut-up dried apricots, or cut-up dried apples.

Apple, Oatmeal, and Coconut Muffins

Not too sweet and packed with nutrients, these muffins are a great take-along midmorning snack. If a recipe like this one calls for a mixture to stand for 10 minutes, I use the time to put away the ingredients I no longer need, to clean the dirty utensils, and to work ahead (in this case, I mix the flour, baking powder, and cinnamon).

MAKES 12 MUFFINS

2 cups chopped apples (peeled or unpeeled)
1 cup rolled oats
1 cup low-fat plain yogurt
⅔ cup honey
⅓ cup shredded unsweetened coconut

⅓ cup extra-light-tasting olive oil
1 egg
1½ cups whole wheat flour
2 teaspoons baking powder
2 teaspoons ground cinnamon
¼ teaspoon ground cloves

1. Preheat the oven to 375°F. Spray a muffin pan with vegetable spray, or place baking cups in the muffin pan.

2. Combine the apples, oats, yogurt, honey, coconut, and oil in a mixing bowl. Mix well. Let the mixture stand for 10 minutes. Add the egg and mix thoroughly.

3. In another mixing bowl, combine the flour, baking powder, and spices and mix well. Add to the oat mixture and stir until the dry ingredients are moistened.

4. Fill the muffin cups; they will be quite full. Bake for 25 minutes or until a wooden toothpick inserted into the middle of a muffin comes out clean. Cool the muffins in the pan for 5 minutes, then remove from the pan and let cool completely.

VARIATION: Add ¼ cup of raisins to the batter with the egg.

Squash Corn Muffins

Cooked squash gives these corn muffins some moisture and some vitamins to boot. Cooked pumpkin can be substituted. I use some white flour here because the results with all whole wheat flour are a little too dense.

MAKES 12 MUFFINS

¾ cup cornmeal

¾ cup whole wheat flour

½ cup unbleached all-purpose flour

2½ tablespoons dry buttermilk powder

1 tablespoon baking powder

½ teaspoon salt

½ teaspoon ground cinnamon

¼ teaspoon ground cloves

⅔ cup light brown sugar

¼ cup unsalted butter, cut in pieces

2 eggs

2 tablespoons honey

¾ cup pureed cooked squash (or pumpkin)

⅔ cup water

1. Preheat the oven to 350°F. Spray a muffin pan with vegetable spray, or place baking cups in the muffin pan.

2. In a large bowl combine the cornmeal, whole wheat flour, white flour, buttermilk powder, baking powder, salt, cinnamon, and cloves. Mix well.

3. Place the sugar, butter, eggs, and honey in a food processor fitted with the steel blade. Blend until smooth. Add the squash and water and mix well. Add the squash mixture to the flour mixture and mix well with a long-handled spoon.

4. Spoon the batter evenly into the 12 muffin cups and bake for 20 minutes, or until a wooden toothpick inserted in the center of a muffin comes out clean. Let the muffins cool for a few minutes and then remove from the pan and cool completely.

Sour Cream Muffins

These are a little indulgent because of the butter, but if you do the math, you'll discover that you still get less than 1 tablespoon per muffin. To compensate for this much butterfat, I use reduced-fat sour cream. These muffins are so delicious you won't need any butter or jam on them at all, so you save the calories on the back end.

MAKES 12 MUFFINS

1 cup dates
1 cup unbleached all-purpose flour
½ cup whole wheat flour
1 teaspoon baking powder
1 cup light brown sugar
½ cup unsalted butter, cut into pieces
2 eggs
1 cup reduced-fat sour cream
1 teaspoon vanilla extract

1. Preheat the oven to 325°F. Spray a muffin pan with vegetable spray, or place baking cups in the muffin pan.

2. Cut the dates into small pieces the size of raisins and set aside.

3. In a large bowl mix the flours and baking powder.

4. Combine the brown sugar and butter in a food processor. Process until well mixed. Add the eggs, sour cream and vanilla, and the flour mixture, processing after each addition until well blended. Scrape down the sides, add the dates, and process again until just mixed.

5. Spoon the batter into the baking cups. Bake for 20 to 25 minutes or until a wooden toothpick inserted in the center of a muffin comes out clean. Let the muffins cool in the pan for a few minutes. Then remove and let cool completely.

Carrot Blondies

These sweet little bites have loads of carrot in them, so they will give you a respectable dose of vitamin A in every bite. These blondies come out flat like pan brownies. I like them best split open like a scone with some cream cheese in the middle.

MAKES 18 BLONDIES

2 eggs
½ cup extra-light-tasting olive oil
½ cup honey
½ teaspoon ground cinnamon
⅔ cup whole wheat flour
⅔ cup unbleached white flour
2 teaspoons baking powder
2 cups shredded carrots (approximately 3 carrots)

1. Preheat oven to 350°F. Grease and flour a 9-by-13-inch pan.

2. Put the eggs in a food processor fitted with the steel blade and blend. Add the oil and honey and process until well blended. Add the cinnamon, flours, and baking powder and blend.

3. Place the flour mixture in a large bowl. Add the carrots and mix well. Pour the mixture in the baking pan and spread out gently.

4. Bake for 25 minutes or until a wooden toothpick inserted in the middle comes out clean. Let cool in pan, then cut into squares.

Orange and Carrot Muffins

A sweet muffin that packs a respectable nutritional punch with fiber, fruits, and a vegetable. Even if you don't ordinarily eat prunes, try them in this recipe; they are sweet like raisins, but they give you a different set of nutrients. You can also cut up pieces of apricots or apples for some variation.

MAKES 12 MUFFINS

1 cup grated carrots
1 banana, mashed
½ cup cut-up prunes or raisins
2 eggs
⅓ cup extra-light-tasting olive oil
⅓ cup honey
1 cup orange juice
1 teaspoon orange extract
2 cups whole wheat flour
¼ cup oat bran
2 teaspoons baking powder

1. Preheat the oven to 375°F. Spray a muffin pan with vegetable spray, or place baking cups in the muffin pan.

2. In a large mixing bowl, place the grated carrots, banana, and prunes. Mix well. Add the eggs, oil, and honey. Mix well. Add the juice and orange extract. Mix well.

3. In a separate bowl, combine the flour, oat bran, and baking powder. Mix well. Add to the carrot mixture and blend together until the dry ingredients are moistened.

4. Divide the batter evenly among the 12 muffin cups. Bake for 25 minutes.

5. Cool muffins a few minutes in the pan, then turn out and let cool completely.

Peanut Butter Bars

These are not low in fat or calories, but they are very filling, so a little goes a long way. As an added benefit, your house will smell heavenly when you bake them. They freeze well.

MAKES 12 BARS

⅔ cup light brown sugar
½ cup peanut butter, smooth or chunky
4 tablespoons unsalted butter, softened
2 eggs
1½ teaspoons vanilla extract
¾ cup whole wheat flour
1½ teaspoons baking powder

1. Preheat oven to 350°F. Grease a 9-by-9-inch pan.

2. Combine the sugar, peanut butter, butter, eggs, and vanilla in a food processor fitted with a steel blade. Blend until well mixed.

3. Add the flour and baking powder to the peanut butter mixture. Blend until well mixed. The dough will be stiff. Scrape the dough into the prepared pan and carefully spread it out and smooth the top with a spatula.

4. Bake for 20 minutes, or until a toothpick inserted into the center comes out clean.

5. Score the cake into 12 bars. Let the cake cool for a few minutes, and then remove the bars. Let cool completely. Store in an airtight container.

...tter Granola Bars

Just because a commercial bar promises "granola," that does not mean it is healthy for you. Making your own is very little work, and it gives you complete control over the ingredients.

MAKES 10 BARS

1½ cups rolled oats

½ cup oat bran

¼ cup dry nonfat milk powder

½ cup raisins

⅓ cup honey

¼ cup peanut butter

¼ cup extra-light-tasting olive oil

½ teaspoon vanilla extract

1 egg

1. Preheat oven to 350°F. Lightly grease a 9-by-9-inch pan.

2. In a large bowl mix the oats, oat bran, and dry milk. Add the raisins and mix well again, making sure the raisins are separated.

3. In a small saucepan combine the honey, peanut butter, oil, and vanilla extract. Stir the honey mixture well for a few moments over very low heat. Do not let the mixture get hot; you only want to raise the heat a little so that the ingredients will combine easily. Take the saucepan off the heat, add the egg, and mix well.

4. Pour the honey mixture over the oat mixture, and with a wooden spoon blend well until all the dry ingredients are moistened.

5. Pour into the prepared pan and distribute somewhat evenly. Bake for 20 minutes.

6. Score into bars with the edge of a spatula. Let the bars cool in the pan, then invert them onto a plate and cut through to separate the bars. Store in an airtight container.

VARIATION: Try this with almond butter and extract.

Apricot Bars

The afternoon I first made these bars, my teenage son and his best friend popped in for a few minutes. Not enough time to tell me how their day had been, but plenty of time to take a bite, mumble approval, and then take a baggie filled with them on their travels.

MAKES 24 BARS

1 cup dried apricots

1 cup rolled oats

½ cup sesame seeds

½ cup unsalted butter, slightly softened, cut in slices

1 cup light brown sugar

2 eggs

1 cup whole wheat flour

1 teaspoon baking powder

1 teaspoon ground cinnamon

1. Preheat the oven to 350°F. Grease a 9-by-13-inch baking pan.

2. Put the apricots and oats in a food processor fitted with the steel blade and process until the oats are cut into ⅛-inch pieces. Put the apricot mixture into a bowl, add the sesame seeds, and mix.

3. Process the butter and sugar until smooth. Add the eggs and process until smooth. Add the flour, baking powder, and cinnamon to the butter mixture and process until well mixed. Finally, add the apricot mixture and process, pulsing on and off until well blended. The batter will be stiff.

4. Spread the batter in the prepared pan and smooth out without compressing too much. Bake for 25 minutes. Cool in pan for 5 minutes. Cut 24 bars, remove, and let cool completely. Store in an airtight container in the refrigerator.

VARIATION: Replace the apricots with equal amounts of other dried fruits.

Soda Bread Scones

Make these once and if you like them as much as my tasters did, pre-mix the dry ingredients in plastic bags and freeze them. That way you only have to add shortening and a little water and you can have fresh scones in 35 minutes. Be sure to write the instructions on a piece of paper and include them on or in the bag! Do not handle or knead the dough too much; the less you do the lighter and fluffier the scones.

MAKES 6 SCONES

1 cup white flour
1 cup whole wheat flour
2 tablespoons dry buttermilk powder
1 tablespoon light brown sugar
1½ teaspoons baking powder
½ teaspoon baking soda
½ teaspoon salt
4 tablespoons unsalted butter, cut into half-teaspoon-size pieces
¾ cup water

1. Preheat the oven to 375°F. Take out a nonstick cookie sheet.

2. Sift together the dry ingredients and pour into a food processor fitted with a steel blade. Add the butter pieces and process about 10 seconds, or until the butter pieces are the size of a lentil.

3. Add the water all at once and process for a few seconds (don't try to get it all mixed perfectly). Turn the dough onto a board and quickly finish the mixing, without too much kneading.

4. Make 6 scones and place them on the cookie sheet. Bake for 25 to 30 minutes.

VARIATION: Add ½ cup currants, raisins, or other cut-up dried fruit when you add the water.

Sweet Potato Biscuits

If you are going to bake a sweet potato for dinner anyway, bake a second one so you can make these biscuits to enjoy the next day. These moist, slightly sweet biscuits are great with a little apple butter.

MAKES 12 TO 16 BISCUITS

1½ cups whole wheat flour

1 cup unbleached all-purpose flour

¼ cup unsalted butter, cut into little pieces

2 tablespoons dry buttermilk powder

4 teaspoons baking powder

1 teaspoon salt

1 cup cooked sweet potato

½ cup water

4 teaspoons honey

½ teaspoon orange extract

1. Preheat the oven to 400°F. Take out a nonstick cookie sheet.

2. Combine the whole wheat flour, white flour, butter, buttermilk powder, and salt in a food processor fitted with a steel blade. Process until the butter is reduced to pea-size pieces. Pour the flour mixture into a large mixing bowl.

3. Process the sweet potato, water, honey, and orange extract until well mixed. Pour the sweet potato mixture into the flour mixture and blend by hand until the dough holds together.

4. Turn the dough onto a lightly floured board and roll out to about ¾ inch (or pat it flat with the heel of your hand). With an overturned glass, cut out the biscuits until all the dough is used up. Place the biscuits on the cookie sheet and bake for 11 to 13 minutes or until they are done.

VARIATION: Try lemon extract for a refreshing difference.

Salads

ommon sense, history, and science agree at least on this much: Fruits and vegetables are vital for radiant health, abundant energy, and appropriate weight. And they are delicious to boot.

With so much new information coming out these days, you could easily be confused about which vegetables and fruits you ought to eat. It is really not necessary to know what contains lycopene and how to tell your anthocyanins from your zeaxanthin! What you do need to do is make sure that you eat a good variety of fruits and vegetables.

Dr. David Heber, in a brilliant book titled *What Color Is Your Diet?* (HarperCollins, 2002), has divided fruits and vegetables into seven color categories, with each color providing a specific and distinctive set of nutrients. The colors indicate the sorts of nutrients the fruits and vegetables will provide. Every day include one fruit or vegetable from each group in your diet, and you'll be sure to get a good variety of nutrients.

The *Red Group* includes tomatoes, pink grapefruit, and watermelon.

In the *Red/Purple Group,* you find purple grapes, prunes, cranberries, red beets, red bell pepper, red apples, strawberries, and blueberries.

The *Orange Group* has pumpkins, carrots, sweet potatoes, mangoes, apricots, and cantaloupes.

Oranges, tangerines, peaches, lemons, pineapple, papayas, and nectarines belong to the *Orange/Yellow Group*.

Yellow/Green is a diverse group that includes green peas, green beans, spinach, green peppers, cucumbers, kiwi, honeydew, zucchini, corn, and avocados.

Garlic, onions, celery, leeks, and mushrooms belong to the *White/Green Group*.

The *Green Group* contains vegetables such as broccoli, cabbage, and bok choy.

Five-Ingredient Salads: From Artichokes to Zucchini

With just five ingredients you can make wonderfully varied salads. On the following pages is a collection to try, and then you can go on to experiment with combining other fruits and vegetables, mixing up batches of different dressings, and adding little bits of "extras," such as nuts, pickled vegetables, olives, and cheeses. Just be aware that the more "extras" you add, the more calories you'll consume. The recipes for the dressings are at the end of this section. Though I highly advocate that you make your own dressings, you can, of course, use bottled varieties if you like them.

You can make your lunch salad the night before, so it is ready to go in the morning. Just be sure to pack it in an airtight container to preserve flavors. I like packing my dressing separately, because I think the flavors remain fresher. There are very small containers that allow you to pack small quantities of dressing.

Artichokes

If you eat artichokes at home, there is no reason why you cannot bring them to work. It is in part because it takes some time to eat whole artichoke that they are so useful: It takes 20 minutes for your brain to register that you are full, so eating a "slow" vegetable allows you the time to feel full.

Be sure to clip all the sharp pointy ends off the artichoke leaves. Boil the artichokes until they are soft, about 40 minutes. Pull off the leaves, dip the meaty ends of the leaves in a sauce, and suck and scrape off the soft bottom half of the leaf with your teeth. You'll have to take out the last few light yellow leaves and the fuzzy and prickly choke portion with a spoon. Once that is gone, the delicious artichoke bottom is left. Though the traditional dipping sauce is melted butter, any kind of lower-fat dipping sauce or salad dressing can be used.

Artichokes supply vitamins A and C as well as potassium.

Artichoke, Beet, and Carrot Salad

SERVES 1

3 artichoke hearts, packed in oil, chopped
½ small, uncooked, red beet, grated
½ carrot, grated
¼ cup feta cheese
1 cup spinach leaves
Basic Vinaigrette (see page 67)

Mix the artichokes, beet, carrot, and feta cheese. Serve on a bed of spinach with the vinaigrette.

Asparagus

Although this is traditionally a spring vegetable, it now is available throughout the year. Snap the tough bottoms off a fresh asparagus spear before lightly steaming the spears. After you have steamed asparagus for dinner, you can place some of the spears in a plastic bag for lunch the next day. Pack a small container of salad dressing with it. Or you can pour Italian dressing over cut-up steamed asparagus for a tasty and healthy salad. You also can place steamed asparagus in a nori roll for a special treat.

Asparagus is a good source of vitamins A and C and has a little calcium and iron.

Asparagus Salad

SERVES 1

6 spears asparagus, cooked, cut into 1-inch pieces
¼ cup finely diced red bell pepper
¼ cup finely diced zucchini
1 tablespoon minced red onion
1 hard-boiled egg, mashed
Honey Mustard Vinaigrette (see page 68)

Mix the asparagus, bell pepper, zucchini, and onion. Sprinkle mashed hard-boiled egg on top. Serve with the Honey Mustard Vinaigrette.

Avocado

Avocado is a mild vegetable that when mashed up to a smooth paste and flavored with a little salt and pepper is a perfect and nutritious spread. Always include a little lemon juice in an avocado dish, so that it will keep its bright green color. Try making a flour tortilla wrap with mashed avocado, chopped cucumbers, sprouts, tomatoes, and refried beans.

Avocados are the highest vegetable source of vitamin E.

Avocado Shrimp Salad

SERVES 1

1 cup mixed baby greens
½ avocado, peeled and cut in slices
½ grapefruit, peeled and in sections
½ tomato, cut in sections
¼ cup cooked shrimp
Creamy Vinaigrette (see page 68)

On top of the baby greens, arrange the avocado slices, the tomato slices, and the grapefruit sections. Sprinkle the shrimp over all. Serve with Creamy Vinaigrette.

Beans

Green beans, also known as string beans or French beans, are an ideal vegetable, if you ask me. They are perfect dipping vegetables. Lightly steamed they are crunchy and a pretty green color and will keep for a few days. Because they are great in so many dishes, you can steam a lot of them at the beginning of the week and then add them to dishes all during the week as well as use them for lunch. They are great to stuff in wraps because of their shape.

Beans are available all during the year. Their cousin, the yellow wax bean, is available mainly in the summer.

Green beans supply vitamin A and potassium.

Shelling beans, such as fava beans and lima beans, is a fun job while you are curled up on the couch watching an old movie. They are great additions to any mixed salads. Try mixing them with chopped tomatoes and crumbled feta cheese and sprinkle some oregano over all. You can also eat them raw as a delicious snack.

Dried beans come in many varieties. They can find their way into many dishes: garbanzo beans in hummus, split peas in soup, pinto beans in a Mexican dip. You might find the beans more digestible if you throw away the soaking water for the dried beans before you cook them in fresh water.

If you want to make a pretty and easy kitchen gift, you can layer different beans in a glass container. Add a recipe for bean soup and a pretty ribbon and you have a great homemade gift.

Shell beans and dried beans are a great vegetarian source of protein as well as iron and potassium.

If you want to grow a highly nutritious food, grow bean sprouts. There are excellent books on sprouting by Steve "the sprout man" Meyerowitz that I highly recommend. Tuck sprouts into salads, sandwiches, and pita pockets for a wonderful burst of health.

Green Bean and Pear Salad

SERVES 1

2 cups steamed green beans, cut in 1-inch sections

1 pear, peeled, seeded, and chopped

¼ cup chopped macadamia nuts

¼ cup minced red pepper

2 cups mixed baby lettuces

Fruit Salad Dressing (see page 68)

Mix the green beans, pear, nuts, and red pepper. Serve over greens with the dressing.

Beets

Beets are packed with healthful components, such as folate, a B vitamin. They have a sweet and mild taste. Don't spill them on your clothes, though; they leave an almost permanent red stain.

Beet Salad

SERVES 1

½ cup grated uncooked beets

½ cup grated carrot

½ cup grated apple

½ cup grated cabbage

2 tablespoons chopped walnuts

Balsamic Vinaigrette (see page 67)

Mix the beets, carrots, apples, cabbage, and walnuts. Dress with the vinaigrette.

Broccoli and Cauliflower

Raw or lightly steamed broccoli and cauliflower are easy vegetables to like. They are great for dipping, good in a chopped salad, and delicious in a cream soup.

A few small white or green florets provide you with vitamins A and C. They also help to protect against some types of cancer.

Broccoli and Cauliflower Salad

SERVES 1

½ cup broccoli, lightly steamed
½ cup cauliflower, lightly steamed
½ cup cooked sliced carrots
¼ cup alfalfa sprouts
3 tablespoons slivered almonds
Creamy Vinaigrette (see page 68)

Mix the broccoli, cauliflower, carrots, sprouts, and almonds. Serve with Creamy Vinaigrette.

Cabbage

Though cooked cabbage is not a popular food, we all gladly eat it raw in coleslaw. Shredded cabbage is also a great addition to tomato-based soups; the tomato somehow mellows out the assertive taste of the cabbage.

It is worth making an effort to add cabbage to various salads, soups, and sandwiches because it has such powerful health-giving properties. It is a good source of vitamin C and fiber.

Cabbage Salad

SERVES 1

¾ cup shredded cabbage

¼ cup shredded carrot

¼ cup shredded Granny Smith apple

¼ cup chopped raw cranberries

2 tablespoons shelled pumpkin seeds

Honey Mustard Vinaigrette (see page 68)

Mix the cabbage, carrot, apple, and cranberries. Sprinkle the seeds on top. Serve with the vinaigrette.

Carrots

This versatile vegetable can either be the star of, or play a great supporting role in, a wide variety of dishes. Baby carrots are easy to dip in dressing; grated carrot is usually a nice addition to a salad or sandwich; chopped carrots work well in many soups; and it is one of the few vegetables that can find its way into desserts.

Carrots supply great amounts of beta-carotene and vitamin A and are the traditional protectors of our eyesight.

Sweet Carrot Salad

SERVES 1

1 cup finely grated carrot
½ cup shredded zucchini
½ cup mango in small chunks
½ cup chopped green grapes
¼ cup pecans
Fruit Salad Dressing (see page 68)

Mix the carrot, zucchini, mango, grapes, and pecans. Serve with the dressing.

Celery

Together with carrots, celery is a favorite vegetable for dipping. Because of its reliable, wilt-proof crunch, it is also a great addition to chicken and turkey salads. Celery gives you vitamin C and potassium.

Celery Salad

SERVES 1

½ cup chopped celery
½ cup halved purple grapes
½ cup papaya in small chunks
½ cup goat cheese
¼ cup shelled sunflower seeds
Fruit Salad Dressing (see page 68)

Gently mix the celery, grapes, papaya, goat cheese, and sunflower seeds. Serve with Fruit Salad Dressing.

Corn

There are so many wonderful ways to eat this vegetable, just use your imagination. Not only is it delicious on its own, it is also an excellent addition to salads and soups. Though it is easy to grab for frozen and canned corn, it is actually very easy to scrape the kernels from leftover steamed corn on the cob. Much tastier and healthier too! It is a good source of vitamin C.

Corn and Cilantro Salad

SERVES 1

1 cup cooked fresh corn kernels
½ tomato, finely chopped
¼ cup minced green pepper
¼ cup chopped black olives
2 tablespoons minced fresh cilantro
Basic Vinaigrette (see page 67)

Mix the corn, tomato, pepper, olives, and cilantro. Top with the vinaigrette.

Cucumbers

Cukes are loved for their cool crunch with a mild flavor. You can cut them into spears, discarding the seeds in the middle, so they can be finger foods. Lots of people use them sliced in tossed salads, but they also make a delicious salad on their own. They are a good source of vitamin C.

Middle Eastern Cucumber Salad

Some variation of this salad is often eaten for breakfast in Middle Eastern countries. There it is tossed with a little bit of oil and vinegar or dressed with a little yogurt.

SERVES 1

½ cup chopped cucumber

½ cup chopped tomato

½ cup chopped green pepper

2 tablespoons minced green olives

1 tablespoon minced scallion (white part)

Basic Vinaigrette (see page 67)

Mix the cucumber, tomato, pepper, olives, and scallion. Serve with the vinaigrette.

Greens

I hate to be the one to say something bad about a vegetable, but there is really next to nothing good that can be said about iceberg lettuce, however popular it is. The healthful benefits of lettuce are in the dark green–colored part, and the anemic color of iceberg should tell you that it is the vegetable equivalent of white sugar. Experiment with the many dark green lettuces that you can find in the market. Try crunchy romaine, deep green spinach, buttery Boston, peppery watercress, and the mixed baby lettuces that are now common in supermarkets. You might also like to get adventurous and chop up kale, mustard greens, and other dark green leaves that are more commonly eaten cooked.

Green leaves can serve a great role in a sandwich by providing a waterproof barrier between bread and a filling such as tuna fish, which could otherwise turn the bread soggy. Wash lettuce leaves at one go, and store the dried leaves loosely in a plastic bag for a few days. That way you will always have them ready for lunch and dinner.

Greens are good sources of vitamin A and fiber and the amazingly beneficial chlorophyll.

Green Green Salad

SERVES 1

1 cup mixed baby greens
1 cup fresh spinach leaves
½ cup fresh snow peas
1 tablespoon minced fresh basil
1 tablespoon minced fresh parsley
Basic Vinaigrette (see page 67)

Mix the baby greens and spinach. Sprinkle the snow peas on top. Sprinkle the fresh herbs over all. Top with the vinaigrette.

Peas and Snow Peas

Shelling peas is fun, just pull the string and find all those peas snugly nestled in the pod. You can even take unshelled peas with you to work. If they are fresh and small, they are delicious raw.

Snow peas can be eaten uncooked and are about the easiest vegetable to tuck into a lunch bag. With a little goat cheese, they make a super easy snack.

Peas are chock-full of vitamins A and C and various B vitamins.

Peas and Carrots Salad

SERVES 1

¾ cup fresh, uncooked, shelled peas

½ cup carrots cut into little cubes, roughly the size of the peas

¼ cup finely minced red pepper

1 tablespoon minced fresh dill

1 tablespoon minced leek

Dill Vinaigrette (see page 67)

Mix the peas, carrots, red pepper, dill, and leek. Serve with Dill Vinaigrette.

Peppers

Bell peppers come in red, green, yellow, black, and orange. Chopped peppers make a colorful addition to any salad. Peppers can also be cut into strips and dipped into dressing. Red peppers have a milder and sweeter taste than green ones. Bell peppers give us vitamins C and B_6.

Triple Pepper Salad

SERVES 1

¼ cup minced green pepper

¼ cup minced red pepper

¼ cup minced yellow pepper

2 tablespoons minced fresh cilantro

2 tablespoons chopped pumpkin seeds

Creamy Vinaigrette (see page 68)

Mix the three kinds of peppers, cilantro, and seeds. Serve with Creamy Vinaigrette.

Potatoes and Sweet Potatoes

Potatoes are usually classified as a starch, but they are, of course, a root vegetable. They cannot be eaten raw, but they are a great leftover once they are cooked. Bell peppers, radishes, celery, peas, carrots, and corn can all be mixed in a potato salad to make it more nutritious and flavorful. Potatoes are high in vitamin C and potassium.

Sweet potatoes supply excellent quantities of vitamin A and can be substituted for regular potatoes in many recipes. Cooked and cubed sweet potatoes can be tossed with orange sections and dressed with balsamic vinegar dressing for an unusual salad.

Potato and Red Pepper Salad

SERVES 1

1 cup diced cooked potatoes

⅓ cup chopped red pepper

2 tablespoons minced chives

2 tablespoons chopped walnuts

2 tablespoons minced fresh parsley

Russian Dressing (see page 103)

Mix the potatoes, red pepper, chives, walnuts, and parsley. Serve with Russian Dressing.

Radishes

Red, round, cute, and squishproof in a lunch bag, radishes have a little bit of a bite to them. They are a good source of vitamin C.

Radish Crunch Salad

SERVES 1

½ cup chopped radishes

½ cup chopped celery

½ cup chopped apple

2 tablespoons minced fresh basil

1 tablespoon minced scallion

Italian Vinaigrette (see page 67)

Mix the radishes, celery, apple, basil, and scallion. Serve with Italian Vinaigrette.

Tomatoes

Tomatoes are one of the most popular vegetables. Fresh tomatoes are great sliced on sandwiches or chopped in salads, and cherry tomatoes you can just pop into your mouth! Cherry tomatoes are also great on skewers, or you can cut off the cap, scoop out the inside with a melon scooper, and stuff it with a little flavored cream cheese, tuna salad, or chicken salad. Place the cap back on and you have a little cherry tomato surprise!

Tomatoes supply vitamins A, C, and E.

Tomato Mozzarella Salad

SERVES 1

1 cup chopped tomatoes
¼ cup diced mozzarella cheese
2 tablespoons minced fresh basil
2 tablespoons minced red onion
1 cup fresh spinach
Basic Vinaigrette (see page 67)

Mix the tomatoes, cheese, basil, and red onion. Serve over spinach leaves with the vinaigrette.

Zucchini

You can mix this mild-mannered raw vegetable into lots of different salads because it lends a mild crunch. It is also good with a dip. Zucchini is high in vitamin C.

Zucchini Salad

SERVES 1

1 cup chopped zucchini
½ cup fresh green peas
½ cup cubed sharp cheddar
2 tablespoons chopped walnuts
1 tablespoon minced fresh dill
Creamy Vinaigrette (see page 68)

Mix the zucchini, peas, cheddar, walnuts, and dill. Serve with Creamy Vinaigrette.

Salad Dressings

Basic Vinaigrette

I can see no reason why you would buy ready-made dressing. I once went to a huge food show where they gave people the opportunity to try fifty different dressings. I did not taste one that was as good as my own, plain vinaigrette. And there are so many mustards and vinegars that no two batches need to taste the same.

You can whip up this vinaigrette in five minutes. If I think I will use it up in about five days, I leave it out at room temperature. But for longer periods of time, I refrigerate it. When the vinaigrette gets cold, the olive oil has a tendency to get semisolid, so be sure to take it out before you plan to use it to get it back to room temperature. Give it a good shake to mix up the ingredients.

MAKES 1 CUP

½ cup extra-virgin olive oil
¼ cup apple cider vinegar
¼ cup Dijon mustard (more or less to taste)
1 small clove garlic (more if you like the taste of garlic)
Salt and pepper to taste

Put all the ingredients in a jar. Cover and shake well. Or blend in a blender for a longer emulsification.

VARIATIONS: *Italian Vinaigrette:* Add 1 teaspoon dried oregano and ½ teaspoon dried thyme.

Dill Vinaigrette: Add 2 tablespoons fresh minced dill (use dill mustard if you have it).

Balsamic Vinaigrette: Instead of cider vinegar, use balsamic vinegar and reduce the mustard to 1 tablespoon.

Honey Mustard Vinaigrette: Instead of Dijon mustard, use honey mustard.

Blue Cheese Vinaigrette: Add ¼ cup blue cheese to taste (you'll need to make this in the blender). Reduce the mustard to 1 tablespoon.

Creamy Vinaigrette: Use rice vinegar instead of apple cider vinegar and add 1 to 2 tablespoons mayonnaise instead of the mustard.

Fruit Salad Dressing

A sweet dressing perfect for any green salad with fruits.

MAKES ½ CUP

¼ cup coconut oil
2 tablespoons fresh lemon juice
1 tablespoon honey
¼ teaspoon tamari

Place all ingredients in a jar, cover tightly, and shake until well blended.

Other Salads

Chef's Salad

A chef's salad is a great way to use up small quantities of lettuce and meats, cheese, and egg. There is no set recipe for this; just use up the little bits you have in the refrigerator.

SERVES 1

Lettuce

Tomato

Cucumber

Cold cuts

Cheese

Hard-boiled egg

Dressing of your choice

Layer the ingredients, in order listed, in a container. Pack the dressing separately.

Chicken Salad

With the crunch of the celery and the sweetness of the grapes, this chicken salad is popular with all ages. If you are watching your calories, make it with low-fat yogurt instead of mayonnaise. If you're using this for a sandwich filling, line the bread with lettuce leaves so that it does not become soggy.

SERVES 2

1 chicken breast, cooked

½ cup chopped celery

½ cup chopped grapes

1 teaspoon mayonnaise

1 teaspoon Basic Vinaigrette
 (see page 67)

½ teaspoon dried rosemary

Blend all ingredients in a large bowl. Chill in an airtight container.

Greek Salad

Salads are sometimes easier to eat if all the ingredients are shred-ded finely. Quantities are, of course, really flexible and depend entirely on appetite. I don't like adding croutons to any salad because after a very short time they become soggy. So I make large croutons from leftover bread and pack them separately.

SERVES 1

3 leaves romaine lettuce, shredded
½ tomato, finely chopped
¼ cucumber, finely chopped
2 tablespoons minced red onions
2 tablespoons feta cheese, crumbled
½ teaspoon dried oregano
Italian Vinaigrette (see page 67)
Croutons

1. In a plastic container, layer the ingredients in the order given above. Sprinkle the oregano over all.

2. Pack the vinaigrette separately or moisten the salad with vinai-grette and let it marinate. Before serving, add croutons.

Croutons

Dried-out bread—for instance, crusts or slices of French bread
Olive oil or garlic-flavored olive oil

With a food brush, brush a little of the oil on the bread crusts or slices. Place them on a baking sheet and toast them in the toaster oven or under the broiler. When the bread is nicely browned, care-fully turn over, brush on a little more oil, and toast briefly again. Cool and store in an airtight container.

Tuna Salad Niçoise

You probably have a favorite tuna fish salad recipe by now. But if you are bored with it, here is a delicious, new, vegetable-filled variation inspired by the classic Mediterranean Salad Niçoise. I suggest that you pack it separately, in a plastic container, with a roll on the side.

MAKES 2 CUPS

1 6-ounce can water-packed tuna fish, drained well

1 cup finely chopped celery (about 2 stalks)

½ cup finely chopped red pepper

2 tablespoons chopped black olives

1 tablespoon minced sweet onions

1 tablespoon mayonnaise

1 tablespoon low-fat yogurt

1 teaspoon apple cider vinegar

½ teaspoon salt or to taste

Freshly ground pepper to taste

2 cups torn lettuce leaves

1. Put the tuna fish in a mixing bowl and add the celery, red pepper, olives, and onion. Mix well. Add the mayonnaise, yogurt, vinegar, salt, and pepper. Mix well.

2. Line a plastic container with lettuce leaves and put the salad on top. Pack cold.

Waldorf Salad

This popular salad was created by Oscar Tschirky, headwaiter at the elegant Waldorf-Astoria Hotel in New York City when it opened in 1893. His salad made him so famous that eventually he was listed in *Who's Who!*

Crushed pineapple freezes well. If you think you might like to make this recipe frequently, freeze two-tablespoon portions of pineapple in ice cube containers. Remove the pineapple chunks when they are fully frozen and place them in a marked plastic bag for future use.

If you are using a tart apple, you will need a little less lemon juice. But don't omit the lemon juice completely, since it will prevent discoloration of the apple.

MAKES 1½ CUPS

1 crisp apple
½ to 1 teaspoon fresh lemon juice
1 stalk celery, chopped
¼ cup chopped walnuts
2 tablespoons crushed pineapple
1 tablespoon 1-percent-fat yogurt
1 teaspoon mayonnaise

1. Chop the apple into small chunks, place in a mixing bowl, and sprinkle with the lemon juice. Add the celery, walnuts, and pineapple. Mix well. Store in an airtight container in refrigerator.

2. In a separate bowl, mix the yogurt and mayonnaise. Just before serving, pour dressing over the apple mixture and blend well.

Green Beans Vinaigrette

It is certainly easy enough to steam green beans or use leftover ones and marinate them overnight in a mild rice-vinegar vinaigrette. And they're great to take to work. Just lift them out of the vinaigrette in the morning and place them in a plastic container. Try adding some minced garlic to the vinagrette, or some Vidalia onion or minced red pepper to the beans.

SERVES 2

1/2 pound green beans
1/4 cup olive oil
1 tablespoon rice vinegar
1 tablespoon coarse Dijon-style mustard
1/4 teaspoon salt

1. Put a steamer basket at the bottom of a saucepan and add water up to but not over the bottom of the steamer. Bring the water to a boil.

2. Wash the green beans and cut the tips off the ends. Place the beans in the steamer and cover. Let them steam for about 4 minutes, or until they turn bright green.

3. Meanwhile, put the oil, vinegar, mustard, and salt in a blender and blend until emulsified.

4. When the green beans are done steaming, drain them in a colander. Place the hot beans in a dish and pour the vinaigrette over them, turning the beans to cover them. Let the dish cool to room temperature, then cover it. Let the beans marinate overnight in the refrigerator.

5. To serve, drain the beans and place them in a plastic container for some green finger food. Eat cold or at room temperature.

Vegetable Cheese Pasta Salad

The next time you cook pasta for dinner, cook some extra and make this salad to take to work the next day. There are as many variations on this pasta salad as there are leftovers. You can use any cheese you like, except American cheese; just about any combination of vegetables will do; and you can use other dressings if you prefer. Keep in mind that the real trick to a pretty vegetable pasta salad is to use small pasta shapes and to chop the rest of the ingredients small, so you can get a little of all the different tastes in every forkful.

MAKES 2 CUPS

½ cup dry or 1 cup cooked ditalini or other small pasta shapes
⅓ cup diced red pepper
⅓ cup diced steamed green beans
⅓ cup diced feta cheese
⅓ cup low-fat yogurt
1 tablespoon dry buttermilk powder
1 teaspoon minced fresh oregano
⅛ teaspoon salt

1. Cook the pasta according to the instructions on the package.

2. In a bowl combine the cooked pasta, red pepper, beans, and feta cheese. Mix well.

3. In a small bowl mix the yogurt, buttermilk powder, oregano, and salt. Pour the dressing over the pasta mixture and blend well. Chill.

VARIATIONS: Use cheddar, Monterey Jack, or any other favorite cheese (except American). You can use mozzarella, but the result might be too bland.

Cooked or steamed vegetable choices include asparagus, broccoli, artichoke hearts, and wax beans.

Raw vegetable choices include tomatoes, whole cherry tomatoes, and green peppers.

Dressings you might like to try are balsamic vinaigrette and Russian.

Add a tablespoon of minced Vidalia onion, parsley, dill, or basil to enhance the flavor.

Dilled Cucumber Salad

This will make a tasty salad with soft, wilted cucumbers. It does not matter if you make this the evening before or in the morning; either way you will have enough time for the marinade to do its magic.

SERVES 2

1 cucumber, peeled and sliced thin
2 teaspoons apple cider vinegar
⅓ cup water
1 tablespoon snipped fresh dill
½ teaspoon white sugar
Salt and pepper to taste

1. Combine all the ingredients and let them marinate for at least 1 hour in the refrigerator.

2. Drain off the dressing and serve cold.

Caponata

This sweet-sour dish works well as a salad or piled high on a crispy bread. I like it best at room temperature, because that allows the flavors to blend well, but cold is good too.

MAKES 5 CUPS

2 tablespoons extra-virgin olive oil
1 small onion, minced
3 cloves garlic, minced
1 cup sliced mushrooms
1 medium eggplant
1 28-ounce can crushed tomatoes
1 cup golden raisins
3 tablespoons dried basil
1 teaspoon dried oregano
½ teaspoon salt
2 teaspoons apple cider vinegar
¼ cup minced parsley

1. Heat the oil in a sauté pan. Add the onion and sauté until it is transparent. Add the garlic and sauté for 1 minute. Place the onion and garlic in a large pot. In the same pan, without cleaning it, sauté the mushrooms until they give up their moisture. Add to the large pot.

2. Dice the eggplant into half-inch cubes.

3. Add the eggplant, tomatoes, raisins, basil, oregano, salt, and vinegar to the large pot. Simmer on low heat, uncovered, for 2 hours, stirring occasionally to prevent scorching. Remove from heat and cool to room temperature. It can be chilled overnight to be eaten the next day.

4. Serve warm or cold with parsley sprinkled on top.

Oriental Zucchini-Apple Salad

This unusual salad is based on a Far Eastern recipe. It has a little garlic in it, so be sure to have a toothbrush with you.

SERVES 2

1 tablespoon extra-virgin olive oil

2 small zucchini, sliced

1 apple, peeled, cored, sliced

1 small onion, minced

½ cup walnuts, whole or in pieces

½ cup fresh parsley, stems removed

1 small clove garlic

2 tablespoons olive oil

2 tablespoons low-fat yogurt

Juice of 1 lemon

Salt and pepper to taste

1. Over medium heat, warm the olive oil in a large frying pan. Sauté the zucchini, apple, and onion until they are soft and are beginning to brown. With a slotted spoon, take the vegetables out and let them cool in a bowl.

2. Place the steel blade in a food processor. Add the walnuts and parsley, and process until the walnuts are finely ground. Add the garlic, oil, yogurt, and lemon juice. Process until you have a smooth dressing. Season with salt and pepper to taste.

3. Pour the dressing over the vegetables, mix gently, and refrigerate. Serve cold or at room temperature.

Cold Sesame Noodles

Make some extra spaghetti or other pasta at dinner time and you can have this great lunch ready in a flash. Making this the night before also allows the noodles to soak up the dressing for a bit, though it's not essential. You can substitute apple cider vinegar for the rice vinegar and soy sauce for the tamari, but the result will not be as crisp. Regular sesame oil will not do the trick, so be sure to get Oriental sesame oil to get the full Asian flavor.

MAKES 3 CUPS

3 cups cooked pasta
2 tablespoons tahini
1 tablespoon rice vinegar
1 tablespoon tamari
1 tablespoon water
1 teaspoon Oriental sesame oil
1 scallion, white part and 2 inches of green, finely chopped

1. In a jar mix the tahini, vinegar, tamari, water, and oil.

2. Pour the dressing over the noodles. Mix well. Let the dressing soak in for a while. Then add the scallion. Mix well. Refrigerate if you're holding this overnight.

VARIATIONS: Try adding any one or more of the following:

1 cup cooked, cubed chicken breast or ham.

½ cup chopped peanuts.

1 cup lightly steamed broccoli florets.

1 cup sliced snow peas.

Pesto Vegetable Salad

If you have a favorite pesto recipe, by all means use it. I used bought pesto for this recipe to keep it easy to make.

MAKES 6 CUPS

4 cups cooked small pasta shells

3 large tomatoes, chopped

1 green bell pepper, seeded, diced

¼ small red onion, diced

¼ cup minced fresh parsley

⅓ cup pesto

¼ cup balsamic vinegar

1. Gently mix the pasta, tomatoes, pepper, onion, and parsley. In a separate bowl mix the pesto and vinegar.

2. Pour the dressing over all and mix gently but thoroughly. Refrigerate until serving time.

New Potato Salad

A picnic classic, the potato salad is a great dish. The supermarket/
deli variation is not really the healthiest kind, so make this recipe to
keep control over your nutrition and calories.

You can use my Basic Vinaigrette or Italian Vinaigrette or Dill
Vinaigrette for an herb flavor. Balsamic Vinaigrette will add a little
sweetness and Blue Cheese Vinaigrette a powerful blue cheese flavor. Creamy Vinaigrette is milder in taste and can also be used for a
nice change of pace.

SERVES 2 TO 4

14 small new potatoes, boiled
Vinaigrette (see pages 67–68)

1. Put the potatoes in a bowl. Set aside.

2. Pour $\frac{1}{4}$ cup of vinaigrette over the potatoes, preferably when they
   are still warm, and let them marinate overnight.

VARIATIONS: Try adding any one of the following:

1 chopped hard-boiled egg.

$\frac{1}{4}$ cup shredded cheese.

$\frac{1}{2}$ cup chopped vegetables, such as red pepper, green pepper,

steamed broccoli, tomato, or celery.

$\frac{1}{4}$ cup chopped meat, such as roast beef, salami, ham, turkey,

or chicken.

Vegetable Rice Salad

We have all thrown out little bits of dried-out rice saved from dinner a few nights ago and intended to do "something" with. The easiest way to avoid that is to make this salad right after dinner. Take the leftover rice, add a few chopped vegetables including salad vegetables, moisten it all with some dressing, and mix it up. Place the salad in an airtight container in the fridge, and voilà—lunch for tomorrow is waiting. If you start off with brown rice, you get a nice bit of fiber and vitamin Bs as well.

SERVES 2

1 cup cooked brown rice
1 hard-boiled egg, chopped, or ½ cup chopped cooked chicken
1 cup chopped celery
½ cup chopped cucumber
½ cup low-fat yogurt
¼ cup mayonnaise
1 teaspoon honey mustard

Mix all the ingredients in a bowl and chill.

VARIATION: Instead of the yogurt dressing, moisten the salad with a mild vinaigrette.

Mexican Layered Beans

This is a variation on a popular party dip. If you include lots of veggies, this is actually a very healthy dish that you can eat often. I hesitate to give you proportions because you can make this entirely to your taste. Put it together in a plastic container with a tight-fitting lid. Put some low-fat corn chips (see recipe on page 113) into a baggie for using to scoop.

MAKES 1 OR MORE SERVINGS

Canned pinto beans, drained, and mashed with salt to taste
Red onion, minced
Chopped tomato
Chopped green pepper
Canned corn, drained
Salsa
Shredded cheddar cheese
Reduced-fat sour cream

Layer the ingredients in the order listed in a plastic container.

VARIATION: Mash the pinto beans with some cumin.

Soups

don't think of making soups as a separate cooking chore. To me, it is a way of processing leftovers and scraps to make the next nourishing meal. You can have soup simmering on the stove while you do your evening chores, and suddenly you have a meal that is healthier and faster than you could possibly buy at a fast-food place.

Let me explain my "leftover soup methodology." I keep a plastic bag in the freezer and put in it all clean potato peelings (except the peels that are green), tough dark green leaves from leeks and scallions, carrot scrapings (of course, I wash the carrots thoroughly), large outer celery stalks, parsley stems, mushroom stems, all sorts of other vegetables left over from dinners, and the giblets from the chickens I buy whole (except for the livers, which I freeze separately).

After I have served a roast chicken, for instance, I pick all the remaining meat off the carcass for chicken salad. Then I put the carcass and the vegetables from the plastic bag into a big stockpot with lots of water. I add some bay leaves and some salt and pepper, and I put the pot on the stove over a low flame. After the stock comes to a boil, I let it simmer for 5 minutes and then skim the foam from the surface. I let the stock simmer for a few hours.

Then I take the stock off the heat, let it cool down a bit, and strain the broth. If there was a lot of meat on the chicken carcass, you might want to pick it off, but after being simmered, there will be little flavor left. Throw away the vegetables and giblets (unless your grandmother gave you a good recipe for the giblets!). Cool the broth in a container in the refrigerator. Once it is cold, the chicken fat will have congealed on the top, and you can skim it off. You now have a flavorful, healthy broth that will make every soup or stew you add it to more delicious.

I freeze some of the broth in ice cube trays, and when the cubes are frozen, I place them in a marked plastic bag. That way if I need just a little broth for a dish, I don't need to defrost a big container. The rest goes in one- and two-cup containers to be frozen. Most of the time they, too, get unmolded and stored in a plastic bag in the freezer for later use, such as in Ten Vegetable Soup, Onion and Mushroom Soup, and Lentil Soup (see recipes in this chapter).

Though this is not politically correct, you might want to save the chicken fat once in a while to fry up some chopped onion and the defrosted chicken livers. When the chicken livers are done, you can puree them in a food processor fitted with a steel blade. This pâté, or chopped liver, is delicious on crackers and toast. Just remember: A little goes a long way!

Though it is entirely possible, and delicious, to make straight vegetable broth, the gelatinous aspect of soup comes from simmering bones for a long time; a pure vegetable broth will be thin in comparison.

All the soups in this chapter are ideal for eating for lunch at work. If you have a microwave that you can easily use, by all means take the soup with you cold. If you don't have access to a microwave, then preheat a thermos by letting some boiling water sit in it for a minute or two in the morning. Meanwhile heat the soup. When it's hot, pour out the water and fill the thermos with soup, which will stay nice and hot for the morning.

Cream of Tomato Soup

Because you're using canned tomato sauce in this soup, it's easy to make from scratch in a matter of minutes. The magic of making a perfectly smooth white-sauce base with no additional fat is in the technique: The nonstick pan must already be hot, the flour and milk mixture must be completely mixed, and you must continuously stir the sauce as it is getting thick.

If you prefer a perfectly smooth soup, strain the mixture as you pour it from the blender into the hot pan.

SERVES 1

1 cup milk
1 tablespoon whole wheat flour
½ teaspoon instant vegetable broth powder
½ teaspoon olive oil
¼ cup minced onion
½ cup tomato sauce
Salt and pepper to taste

1. Put the milk, flour, and vegetable broth in a blender and blend until smooth.

2. In a large nonstick frying pan, heat the oil and sauté the onion until transparent and just beginning to brown.

3. Transfer the onion to the milk mixture and blend for 30 seconds while keeping the pan hot on a medium flame. Pour the onion-milk mixture at once into the pan and turn the heat up high. Stir continuously until the mixture comes to a boil.

4. Add the tomato sauce and turn the heat down. Simmer for 5 minutes. Add salt and pepper to taste.

5. Store this in the refrigerator until ready to serve or take to work. It can be reheated in a microwave or at home on the stove and poured into a thermos.

Cream of Corn Soup

See the instructions in the Cream of Tomato Soup recipe for the technique of making a white sauce with no butter. I use white flour in this recipe because the whole wheat leaves little dark flecks in the sauce. Although this recipe is for one serving, it's easy to double, triple, or quadruple it. Just go light on the instant vegetable broth, putting in only half of it while making the soup and then adding the rest of it to taste at the end.

SERVES 1

½ teaspoon olive oil
¼ cup minced onion
¼ cup minced celery
1 cup milk
1 tablespoon white flour
1 teaspoon instant vegetable broth powder
½ cup canned corn, drained

1. In a large nonstick frying pan, heat the oil and sauté the onion and celery until the onion is transparent and just beginning to brown.

2. Meanwhile, put the milk, flour, and vegetable broth powder in a blender and blend until smooth. Add the corn and blend for a few seconds until the corn is in small pieces.

3. Add the corn mixture to the hot pan all at once, turn the heat up to high, and stir continuously while the soup comes to a boil.

4. Turn the heat down and, stirring occasionally, let the soup simmer for 5 minutes. It is now ready to serve or cool before packaging to take to work for lunch.

Comforting Chicken Soup

I told you in the chapter introduction how I make chicken broth from leftovers. Here is a "from scratch" recipe that couldn't be easier! This is the sort of recipe where the proportions of things just don't much matter: Throw in loads of celery if you like it, add a couple of extra garlic cloves, and by all means leave out the carrots or dill if you don't happen to like them.

SERVES 8

4 pounds chicken, cut into pieces, except for the livers
8 cups water
1 teaspoon salt
¼ teaspoon dried thyme
5 whole peppercorns
2 onions, chopped
2 celery stalks, chopped
2 medium carrots, chopped
2 large sprigs fresh dill
⅓ cup minced fresh parsley
2 cloves garlic, chopped

1. Put the chicken, water, salt, thyme, and peppercorns in a large pot. Bring to a boil, turn down the heat, and simmer, covered, for 30 minutes.

2. Add the onions, celery, carrots, dill, parsley, and garlic, and bring the soup back to a simmer. Cook for 20 more minutes.

3. Cool the soup until you can handle the chicken comfortably. Remove the chicken and discard the skin. Pull the meat from the bones and cut it into small pieces. Stir the meat back into the soup. Remove the peppercorns. Set aside to cool.

4. Before eating the soup, skim off surface fat and reheat. Serve with parsley sprinkled on top.

Ten Vegetable Soup

Though I call this Ten Vegetable Soup, it could just as easily be eight or twelve vegetable soup because this is a recipe open to endless variation. Vary the broths between beef, chicken or vegetable, or make the soup with water and add miso or tamari after the soup is finished for a salty broth flavor. Virtually all vegetables and grains can be used, so it is a great way to use up leftovers. The real magic of this soup lies in chopping the vegetables into small ¼-inch pieces, so that you get a mix of several vegetables in every bite.

This is a great dish to make on a weekend when you're having a long heart-to-heart talk in the kitchen. While the broth is simmering, keep chopping and adding, starting with the root vegetables and ending with the herbs. And when it's done, you'll have lots of lunches prepared for the week.

This version is a little hot because of the hot peppers; feel free to omit them if you don't like the heat. Quinoa is an easy-to-digest and high-protein grain. Be sure to rinse it well before you add it to the soup, to get rid of the bitter coating. When it is done, it becomes transparent and has a white ring.

SERVES 8

8 cups water, vegetable or beef broth, or chicken stock

1 cup quinoa, rinsed well

½ teaspoon olive oil

1 onion, chopped

2 cloves garlic, minced

1 large potato, scrubbed clean and chopped

1 large carrot, scrubbed clean and chopped

1 cup chopped green beans

2 celery stalks, chopped

1 red pepper, seeded and chopped

½ green pepper, seeded and chopped

2 jalapeño peppers, seeded and minced

2 scallions, both green and white parts, chopped

½ cup minced fresh parsley

1 tablespoon dried oregano

1½ teaspoons dried basil leaves

Salt and pepper to taste

Miso or tamari (optional)

1. Measure the water or broth into a large stockpot and set it over moderate heat. Add the quinoa and stir.

2. Meanwhile, in a small pan heat the oil and sauté the onion until it is transparent. Add the garlic and sauté until the garlic is fragrant, about 1 minute. Add the garlic-onion mixture to the stockpot.

3. Add the potato, carrot, green beans, celery, red pepper, green pepper, jalapeño pepper, scallions, parsley, oregano, and basil, one at a time, as you wash, clean, and chop each vegetable.

4. Keep the soup at a low simmer until all the vegetables and quinoa are cooked through. The time will vary and will depend on how small you cut the root vegetables. Add salt, pepper, miso, or tamari to taste.

Tortellini Soup

This soup is one great reason for keeping a bag of frozen tortellini in the freezer. The fresh ginger and the snow peas give the soup a slight Oriental character.

SERVES 6

6 cups chicken broth

1 14-ounce package of frozen cheese tortellini

3 scallions, minced, equal parts white and green

1 carrot, peeled and shredded

2 cups snow peas

1 cup chopped fresh spinach

1 teaspoon shredded fresh ginger

2 tablespoon minced fresh parsley

Salt and pepper to taste

1. Heat the chicken broth in a large soup. When it comes to a rolling boil, stir in the tortellini. When the broth comes back to a boil, let it simmer for 8 minutes.

2. Add the carrot, snow peas, spinach, and ginger. Simmer the soup until the tortellini is done. Add salt and pepper to taste.

3. When serving, sprinkle fresh parsley on top.

Onion and Mushroom Soup

This is a very hearty and filling soup, even though it is low in calories. It freezes well, so you can make portions in advance.

SERVES 6

1 cup thinly sliced onions

½ cup chopped scallions, equal parts green and white

2 tablespoons olive oil

½ cup white wine

6 cups chicken stock

½ teaspoon dried thyme

Freshly ground pepper

6 slices French bread

½ cup grated Parmesan cheese

1. In a large frying pan, over medium heat, sauté the onions and scallions in the olive oil. When they start to get brown, remove them with a slotted spoon and put them in a large pot. Turn the heat up under the same frying pan and add the mushrooms. Sauté until they are soft. Transfer to the large pot.

2. Pour the wine into the frying pan. With a wooden spatula, scrape the bottom of the pan as the wine boils. After a few seconds, pour the wine and all the scrapings into the pot. Add the stock, thyme, and pepper. Bring to a low simmer for 15 minutes.

3. For serving at home, preheat the oven to 350°F. Ladle the soup into 6 ovenproof bowls. Place a slice of French bread on top, and sprinkle with the Parmesan cheese. Place the bowls in the oven and bake until the cheese melts.

4. For eating at work, heat the soup in the microwave and toast the French bread with a little Parmesan on top in a toaster oven.

Lentil Soup

Lentil soup is satisfying and nourishing and very easy to make. It is a great soup to put a few leftover bits and pieces of vegetables in. Serve this with some pita bread and a cucumber salad on the side.

SERVES 4 TO 6

2 teaspoons olive oil

2 carrots, peeled and diced

2 celery stalks, chopped

1 medium onion, chopped

2 cloves garlic, crushed

4 cups chicken broth

2 cups crushed tomatoes

1 cup cooked, chopped spinach

1 cup lentils

1 teaspoon curry powder

1 teaspoon ground cumin

1 teaspoon apple cider vinegar

1 teaspoon Worcestershire sauce

¼ cup sherry

A few drops of Tabasco sauce

2 tablespoons minced fresh basil

1. Warm the oil in a large pot over medium heat. Add the carrots, celery, and onions and sauté. When the onions are soft and starting to brown, add the garlic and sauté for 30 seconds.

2. Add the broth, tomatoes, spinach, lentils, curry powder, cumin, vinegar, and Worcestershire sauce.

3. Simmer over low heat for 45 minutes, or until the lentils are very soft. At the end, add the sherry. Add Tabasco sauce to taste.

4. Serve hot right away with fresh basil sprinkled on top. Or cool, refrigerate portions in microwave-proof containers, and heat until hot.

Split Pea Vegetable Soup

This hearty soup is great on a cold day. I usually make it as a vegetarian meal, but if I have leftover ham I add it at the last minute. The
soup is easy to heat up in the microwave.

SERVES 4

4 cups water

1 cup split peas, rinsed and picked over

1 potato, peeled and cut into ½-inch pieces

1 large carrot, peeled and cut into ½-inch pieces

1 onion, chopped

1 clove garlic, minced

1 bay leaf

1 cup chopped cooked ham (optional)

1. In a large pot, combine the water, peas, potato, carrot, onion, garlic, and bay leaf. Bring to a boil, turn down the heat, and cover.
   Simmer gently for 2 hours, stirring occasionally. You will need to
   lower the heat and stir more often toward the end of the cooking
   time, or else the bottom will scorch. Add more water if you like
   your soup thinner.

2. You will know that the soup is done when the peas are soft. Add
   the optional ham and heat through. Remove the bay leaf before
   serving.

Minestrone

This is really a complete meal when served with a salad on the side. Minestrone freezes well, so make the full amount.

SERVES 8

1 egg

¼ cup milk

½ cup flavored breadcrumbs

1 pound ground beef

1 tablespoon minced fresh parsley

6 cups beef broth

1 28-ounce can crushed tomatoes

2 cups shredded cabbage

1 carrot, chopped

1 stalk celery, chopped

1 pound mushrooms, sliced

1 onion, minced

2 cloves garlic, minced

1 tablespoon dried basil

1 teaspoon dried oregano

2 bay leaves

1 cup uncooked macaroni

Salt and pepper to taste

½ cup Parmesan cheese

1. Put the egg and milk in a medium-size bowl and stir until well mixed. Add the breadcrumbs and mix again. Add the ground beef and parsley and shape into 1-inch balls.

2. In a large soup pot, combine the beef broth, tomatoes, cabbage, carrot, celery, mushrooms, onion, garlic, basil, oregano, and basil leaves and bring to a boil.

3. Add the macaroni and stir well. Cook the soup for 5 minutes, then add the meatballs, stir gently, and bring back to a gentle boil. Cook for 7 minutes or until the macaroni and meatballs are done. Add salt and pepper to taste.

4. Pack into microwave-safe containers. Sprinkle Parmesan cheese on top when serving.

Vegetable Vermicelli Soup

With its abundance of vegetables, this is really a very nutritious soup. If you use low-fat broth, this is also a low-calorie soup. You can, of course, substitute and omit vegetables so that only your favorites end up in the soup. This recipe makes a large pot, but it freezes so well that it makes very little sense to make less.

SERVES 12

8 cups vegetable broth, chicken broth, or beef stock

3 cups tomato juice or vegetable juice

2 onions, quartered

1 clove garlic

3 carrots, peeled, cut to ¼-inch dice

1 large potato, peeled, cut to ¼-inch dice

1 small zucchini, grated

1 cup fresh green beans, cut into 1-inch sections

1 cup frozen peas

1 teaspoon dried oregano

1 cup cooked vermicelli

Salt and pepper to taste

¼ cup minced fresh parsley

1. In a large stockpot, begin to bring the broth to a boil.

2. Meanwhile, put 2 cups of tomato or vegetable juice, onions, and garlic in a blender container, and puree. Add the puree to the broth with the remaining juice. Bring the liquid to a boil.

3. Add the carrots, potato, zucchini, green beans, peas, and oregano. Cook until the vegetables are soft, about 10 minutes. Add vermicelli and heat through. Correct the seasoning with salt and pepper.

4. Serve hot with parsley sprinkled on top. Or cool and refrigerate or freeze for later use. This is easy to reheat in a microwave.

Mulligatawny Soup

Here's a perfect soup to make after a chicken and rice dinner. You can season it to be mild or hot, depending on how much Tabasco sauce you put in.

SERVES 4

4 cups chicken broth
2 tablespoons flour
2 teaspoons curry powder
½ teaspoon ground cumin
¼ cup olive oil
1 medium onion, minced
2 stalks celery, diced
½ cup diced cooked chicken
½ cup cooked rice
½ cup diced Granny Smith apple
1 teaspoon salt
Tabasco sauce to taste
Pinch dried thyme
½ cup milk

1. Put the chicken broth, flour, curry, and cumin in a blender and blend until smooth.

2. Heat the oil in a large frying pan. Sauté the onion and celery until the onion just starts to brown. Add the broth mixture all at once, turn the heat up, and keep stirring until the broth comes to a boil and thickens.

3. Turn the heat down a bit, add the diced chicken, rice, apple, salt, Tabasco, and thyme. Bring to a boil. Add the milk and heat through.

4. Serve it warm with pita bread.

Potato Leek Soup or Light Vichyssoise

People always think vichyssoise is difficult to make, but this recipe couldn't be easier. The only "work" is washing the leeks, which has to be done thoroughly to make sure all the grit and sand are removed.

SERVES 4

2 medium leeks
2 medium potatoes
4 cups chicken or vegetable broth
½ teaspoon salt or to taste

1. Use the white part of the leek and the soft green part. Cut the leek in 1-inch pieces and wash very well to remove all the grit. You should have approximately 2 cups.

2. Peel and cube the potatoes. You should have about 3 cups.

3. Put the leeks, potatoes, and broth in a medium-size saucepan and bring to a boil. Simmer until the potatoes are very soft, about 15 to 20 minutes. Cool slightly.

4. Pour the soup into a blender container and blend until it is completely smooth. Taste the soup and add salt as needed.

Winter Soup

This is a generic recipe that you can adapt in lots of different ways. You can vary the broth, the meat, and the vegetables almost endlessly. Make notes to yourself in the margin of this recipe to remind yourself of how you like the result of your experiments.

The method for thickening the broth may sound more complicated than it is. You can use the same method for making thick sauces and gravy. What I like about it is that it does not require additional fat and it always produces a perfectly smooth result.

If you have no broth, you can always use instant vegetable broth or bouillon cubes.

SERVES 2

2 cups broth
2 tablespoons flour
1 cup cooked mixed vegetables, such as carrots, celery, and onions
1 cup cut-up cooked chicken
2 tablespoons snipped fresh dill

1. Heat 1 cup of broth in a saucepan to boiling.

2. Meanwhile, put the second cup of broth and the flour in a blender and blend until smooth.

3. When the broth is boiling, whirl the blender one more time to make sure all the flour is mixed very well, and pour all at once into the boiling mixture. Immediately start stirring until the mixture comes back to a boil. Turn down the heat and let the mixture simmer for about 5 minutes, stirring occasionally, so that the flour is properly cooked through.

4. Add the vegetables and chicken, heat through, and adjust the seasoning.

5. Sprinkle the dill on top and serve hot.

VARIATIONS: You can replace the second cup of broth with milk or cream for a creamy soup. Be sure to adjust the seasoning in the end, though, because you will probably need to add salt.

If you like your soup thick, increase the flour to 3 tablespoons.

Some other cooked vegetables to add singly or in combination include cauliflower, broccoli, sweet potato, beans, and peas.

You can include some proteins, too, such as cut-up beef, chicken, turkey, ham, sausage, or fish. Just be sure to adjust the broth to match the protein.

Cold Cucumber Soup

This quick cold soup is wonderful for hot days when you don't want to heat up your kitchen.

SERVES 4

2 cucumbers, peeled	¼ cup snipped fresh dill
1 scallion, equal parts white and green	¼ cup chopped fresh parsley
1½ cups low-fat yogurt	Salt, pepper, and paprika to taste

1. Set aside half of one cucumber and half the scallion. Cut the remaining cucumber into chunks.

2. Place the cucumber chunks, the scallion half, the yogurt, dill, and parsley in a blender. Blend until smooth. Pour into a bowl.

3. Finely chop the reserved cucumber. Mince the scallion.

4. Add the cucumber and scallion to the blended soup and mix. Add salt, pepper, and paprika to taste. Chill.

5. Pour into a chilled thermos for lunch.

Gazpacho

This recipe is meant as a guide; you can vary the vegetables and proportions endlessly. It really depends on what you like, and what happens to be fresh at the market. I use Worcestershire sauce, but, again, it is only one of the options. You can also try adding salt and pepper, tamari, or soy sauce.

SERVES 1 TO 2

1 cup tomato juice or vegetable juice

1 tomato, chopped

½ cucumber, peeled and chopped

¼ red pepper, seeded and chopped

2 tablespoons chopped Vidalia onion

½ teaspoon Worcestershire sauce

½ teaspoon apple cider vinegar

Mix all the ingredients and chill until very cold.

VARIATIONS: Add some finely grated carrots or some chopped green pepper.

To make this soup more substantial, you can add some finely chopped leftover cooked chicken, turkey, or roast beef (not traditional ingredients, but if you like it, why not?).

Spreads and Dips

he easiest way to add interest and variety to a plain sandwich is to vary the spread on the bread. There are lots of commercial options, many of which are very high in calories. Butter, margarine, mayonnaise, and high-fat cheese and cream cheese spreads add flavor but at a high caloric cost. Cutting your mayonnaise with low-fat yogurt will save you lots of fat calories and, if you are clever about it, with virtually no reduction of flavor. Making your own flavored cream cheeses, which takes just a few minutes, allows you to make sure that no additives and preservatives get added. If you wish, you can use low-fat or reduced-fat cream cheese.

The best spreads to buy for some variety are the various mustards. My current favorites are dill mustard and honey mustard, but I try new mustards on a regular basis. They tend not to be high in calories and they add a boost of flavor to dressings and sandwiches.

Look in the salad chapter for some easy-to-prepare dressings, which can be used not only for salads but also as dips for cut-up vegetables.

Mayo-Mustard Spread

This super-easy spread is delicious with most lunchmeats and cheeses. Make it once a week so that it will be ready whenever you need it.

MAKES ½ CUP

¼ cup mayonnaise
¼ cup low-fat yogurt
1 teaspoon to 1 tablespoon Dijon mustard (depending on personal preference)

Mix ingredients thoroughly in a bowl. Store in an airtight container in the refrigerator.

VARIATION: Try different kinds of mustard, such as dill mustard or horseradish mustard, for some variety.

Mustard Marmalade

This unusual spread works well on roast beef, smoked turkey, salami, and pastrami sandwiches.

MAKES ½ CUP

¼ cup Dijon mustard
¼ cup marmalade

Mix the mustard and marmalade to make a spread.

Russian Dressing

A friend who was recovering from major surgery was suffering from terrible nausea. It was a huge effort for him to eat, and it was this dressing that pulled him through: As long as the food was dipped in this comfort food it went down nice and easy!

MAKES ¾ CUP

¼ cup mayonnaise
¼ cup low-fat yogurt
¼ cup tomato ketchup

Mix ingredients thoroughly in a bowl. Store in an airtight container in the refrigerator.

VARIATION: For that authentic texture, mix in a tablespoon of minced relish.

Tuna Yogurt Dip

This dip is good as a spread for a wrap with vegetables, or as a dip with carrot sticks.

MAKES 1 CUP

1 6½-ounce can water-packed tuna, drained
½ cup low-fat yogurt
¼ cup chopped green pepper
1 teaspoon prepared horseradish

Mix all the ingredients well. Chill for 2 hours.

Scallion Cream Cheese Spread

You can buy flavored cream cheese, but since you can make your own in just a few minutes, why bother? And that way you can be sure it's fresh and free of preservatives. Use reduced-fat cream cheese if calories are a concern. This recipe doubles easily. Just go lightly on the seasonings and adjust them to your taste.

SERVES 1

2 ounces cream cheese
1 teaspoon finely minced scallion
Scant ¼ teaspoon tamari or soy sauce

1. Place all ingredients in a shallow bowl and mix well. Refrigerate in an airtight container. Will keep for a week.

2. Try this as a spread on a bagel, topped with a slice of tomato. Wrap tight in plastic wrap.

VARIATIONS: Instead of the tomato, add some watercress and cucumbers on the sandwich.

Instead of the tomato, add some shredded carrots, plus sprouts for a great boost of vitamins.

Raisin and Walnut Cream Cheese Spread

I like spreading this on raisin bagels or whole wheat bagels; the natural sweetness of these varieties works well with this cream cheese.

SERVES 1

2 ounces cream cheese

1½ teaspoons honey

1 teaspoon raisins

⅛ teaspoon ground cinnamon

1 tablespoon finely chopped walnuts

Put the cream cheese, honey, raisins, and cinnamon in a shallow bowl and mix well with a fork. Add the walnuts and blend well.

VARIATIONS: You can try other combinations of fruit and nuts such as:

Dried cranberries and chopped hazelnuts, and mace instead of cinnamon.

Dried cut up peaches and chopped pecans, and a pinch of cloves instead of cinnamon.

Dried cut-up crystallized ginger, and almonds and a pinch of cardamom instead of cinnamon.

Pineapple Cream Cheese Spread

This is a very pretty cream cheese with all its little flecks of red pepper. Try it on a bagel with some shredded carrot for fiber and vitamins.

SERVES 1

2 ounces cream cheese
1 tablespoon well-drained, crushed pineapple
1 tablespoon finely minced red pepper

Put the cream cheese, pineapple, and red pepper in a shallow bowl and mix well with a fork.

VARIATIONS: Top the bagel with a slice of drained canned pineapple.

Top the bagel with some strips of roasted red peppers from a jar.

Sardine Cream Cheese Spread

This unusual spread is good not only on bagels but also on other sandwiches and wraps. Because of its full flavor you only need to add some vegetables.

MAKES 1¾ CUPS

1 8-ounce package reduced-fat cream cheese
1 3¾-ounce can sardines in tomato sauce
1 small onion, finely chopped
2 tablespoons lemon juice

Thoroughly process all the ingredients, in a food processor fitted with a metal blade. Scrape down the sides frequently.

Honey Butter

Make your own honey butter in just a few minutes. It's delicious on cinnamon raisin bread in the morning or on a graham cracker for a snack.

MAKES ¾ CUP

½ cup butter, at room temperature
¼ cup honey

Cream together the butter and honey. Store in the refrigerator. Bring to room temperature before spreading.

VARIATIONS: To the honey mixture add any of the following and blend well:

A sprinkle of ground cloves and mace.

A sprinkle of ground cinnamon and nutmeg.

A few drops of vanilla extract and some raisins.

A few drops of orange extract and some cut-up apricots.

A tablespoon of grated carrots.

A tablespoon of finely chopped walnuts, almonds or hazelnuts.

A tablespoon of grated unsweetened coconut.

Cranberry Relish

This sweet relish is useful on turkey and other meat sandwiches. But by adding a little yogurt to it, it can also be used as the base of a dressing for fruit salads. If you buy extra cranberries at Thanksgiving time and freeze them, you can make this relish year-round.

MAKES ¾ CUP

1 cup fresh or frozen cranberries
½ cup light brown sugar
1 tablespoon water

1. Place the cranberries, sugar, and water in a saucepan and bring to a boil. Turn the heat down to a simmer while the cranberries pop, stirring occasionally.

2. When all the berries have popped, take the saucepan off the heat and let the relish cool. Then transfer the relish to a container and refrigerate.

Sweet Peanut Dip

This is an easy sweet dip for fruit, or spread on a piece of toast. Peanut butter is relatively high in calories, so don't go overboard with this. On the other hand, it is a good source of protein. Use this as a dip for pieces of apple, grapes, banana slices, mandarin oranges, baby carrots, or celery. Or try it as a spread on a toasted bagel or graham crackers.

MAKES ¼ CUP

2 tablespoons peanut butter
1 tablespoon dry milk powder
1 teaspoon honey
2 tablespoons boiling water

In a small bowl, mix the peanut butter, milk powder, and honey. Add the boiling water and mix well. Add a little bit more water to get the desired consistency.

VARIATION: Add a little grated carrot, or raisins.

Mushroom Sandwich Spread

This spread works well on dark pumpernickel or hearty peasant bread. Bring along some small French pickles, too. Though this is made with butter, there is not that much fat per serving.

SERVES 6

⅓ cup butter
½ cup scallions, white part only
¾ pound mushrooms, wiped clean and chopped
¼ cup brandy
¼ teaspoon dried thyme
Salt and pepper to taste
1 tablespoon lemon juice

1. In a medium-size frying pan, melt the butter. Add the scallions and sauté until transparent. Add the mushrooms and cook over high heat to evaporate the moisture. Add the brandy, thyme, salt, pepper, and lemon juice. Sauté for 1 minute.

2. Place the steel blade in a food processor. Blend the mushroom mixture until smooth, scraping down the sides frequently. Chill for at least 3 hours before serving.

Spinach Dip

Ever notice how fast the spinach dip is scooped up at parties? It's not just because it is being served in a cute, hollowed-out loaf of bread; it's because it is delicious. So why save it for special occasions only? This is a great dip with all sorts of vegetables, crackers, or croutons. You can easily double this recipe.

SERVES 4 TO 5

5 ounces frozen chopped spinach (half a package)
1 cup reduced-fat sour cream
1 scallion, white part and 2 inches of the green,
    cut into 1-inch pieces
1½ teaspoons Worcestershire sauce

1. Cook the spinach according to package directions. Place the spinach in a colander and squeeze out the moisture.

2. Place the spinach, sour cream, scallion, and Worcestershire sauce into a food processor fitted with a steel blade. Process until the spinach is chopped into small pieces. Scrape down the sides of the bowl and process again to blend well.

3. Place in a covered container in the refrigerator. Take it to work with little carrots or whole wheat crackers.

Blue Cheese Dressing

Blue cheese is not a low-fat food, but this homemade dip is better than the commercial versions. It makes a great accompaniment for raw vegetables such as celery.

MAKES ½ CUP

¼ cup blue cheese
¼ cup nonfat yogurt

1. Place the cheese in a bowl and mash with a fork. Add the yogurt and mix very well. Chill.

2. Package the dressing in a container with a secure top. Wrap celery sticks in plastic wrap. Take to work for a midday snack.

Bean Dip

You might like Mexican foods, but not the hot taste, so buy your salsa to match your preference. This high-protein dip is good with vegetables or some low-fat baked tortilla chips. It can also be used as a spread on wraps.

MAKES 1 CUP

1 cup cooked canned pinto beans, drained
3 ounces salsa
¼ cup reduced-fat sour cream

Place a steel blade in the food processor and blend all ingredients until smooth.

Salsa with Low-Fat Chips

A fresh salsa, served with homemade low-fat tortilla chips, makes a fine addition to a lunch. If you like the heat, you can add more chiles, of course. Taking the peel off the tomatoes is a small extra step, but worth it since it makes the texture of the salsa smoother.

MAKES 2 CUPS

4 tomatoes

¼ cup chopped onion

1 clove garlic

1 tablespoon olive oil

1 tablespoon basil leaves

1 green chile, stem and
    seeds removed

Salt and black pepper

1. Boil 2 quarts of water in a large pot. Carefully place the tomatoes in the boiling water and let them cook for a few minutes, until you can see the skin "pop." Take the tomatoes out of the water and let them cool. Slip the peels off.

2. In a food processor fitted with the steel blade, process the onion, garlic, oil, and basil leaves until smooth. Scrape down the sides. Add the green chile and process until finely mixed.

3. Quarter the tomatoes and add them to the food processor. Process until the mixture is well blended but still coarse.

Low-Fat Chips

Corn tortillas

Olive oil

Cut corn tortillas into sixths and place them in a single layer on a lightly greased (sprayed) cookie sheet. Spray the tortillas lightly with cooking spray or olive oil. Sprinkle lightly with a little salt. Bake at 350°F for 10 minutes or until lightly browned.

Refried Bean Sandwich Spread

Making Mexican-inspired foods at home lets you monitor the quality of the ingredients, making them much lower in fat than the fast-food versions. Cooking beans is a very easy process, though it takes a little time, and cooked beans freeze really well, so I highly recommend that you do that. But canned beans work just as well for this recipe.

This spread is especially good on a whole wheat tortilla, topped with shredded lettuce, chopped tomatoes and cucumbers, salsa, and shredded cheese.

MAKES ABOUT 1 CUP

1 cup cooked pinto or black beans
½ teaspoon ground cumin
¼ teaspoon salt
Dash of hot pepper sauce to taste
Olive oil

1. In a bowl mash the beans, cumin, salt, and hot pepper sauce.

2. Heat the oil in a skillet and fry the bean mixture over moderate heat, stirring often until it is dry and solid. Cool and store in a closed container in the refrigerator.

Hummus

In less than five minutes you can make this spread with good quality, low-fat protein for a fraction of the cost of store-bought.

MAKES 1 1/2 CUPS

1 15-ounce can garbanzo beans
1/4 cup tahini
2 tablespoons lemon juice
1 clove garlic, crushed through a garlic press
Scant 1/8 teaspoon salt or to taste
Reserved garbanzo bean liquid to taste

1. Drain the garbanzo beans, but reserve the liquid.

2. Place the beans, tahini, lemon juice, garlic, and salt in a food processor fitted with the steel blade. Process until smooth. Scrape down the sides.

3. Add reserved garbanzo bean liquid 1 tablespoon at a time, processing after each addition, until you obtain the desired consistency. How much of the reserved liquid you add to get the desired consistency will depend on how well you drained the beans to begin with.

4. Serve as a dip with pita bread or cut-up vegetables, such as miniature carrots or celery sticks. When you make a wrap sandwich, this works perfectly with lots of fresh or lightly steamed vegetables.

VARIATIONS: *Roasted Pepper Hummus:* Add 2 ounces roasted red pepper (from a jar) to the garbanzo beans in the food processor.

Hot Hummus: Add Tabasco or another hot chili sauce to the finished product to taste.

Baba Ganouj

I have been fortunate enough to live in places—Manhattan's Upper West Side and the Berkshires in Massachusetts—where this Lebanese specialty was a common item in the deli case. But if you are not so fortunate, you can make it yourself. I recommend that you bake an eggplant at the same time that you are making something else in the oven (but don't forget it, as I did once!).

Serving this with pita bread is traditional and simple. You can serve it on a plate and scoop it up with pieces of pita bread. Or, to make a pita sandwich, line it first with lettuce leaves and add a generous helping of this spread and lots of vegetables.

> 2 pounds eggplant (one large or two small)
> 3 cloves garlic, minced
> ¼ cup tahini
> ¼ cup freshly squeezed lemon juice
> 2 tablespoons minced fresh parsley
> ½ teaspoon salt or to taste
> Freshly ground pepper to taste

1. Preheat the oven to 375°F.

2. Place the eggplant on a baking sheet and pierce it several times with a fork. Bake for 1 hour or until the whole eggplant is soft and starts to collapse.

3. Remove it from the oven and let cool. Scrape the soft flesh from the skin (discard the skin) and drain in a colander for 30 minutes.

4. Place a steel blade in a food processor. Add the drained eggplant and the rest of the ingredients. Process, scraping down the sides, until you have a smooth paste. Refrigerate until you are almost ready to eat it. The flavor improves if it is served at room temperature.

Sandwiches

andwiches are generally the centerpiece of brown bag lunches, so it is really important that you get the maximum nutrition out of them.

It is usually in your lunchtime sandwich that you will get some protein. It is the protein that will give you the sustained energy you will need for the long afternoon. Eating a carbohydrate-only lunch might make your energy spike and then dip so low that by late afternoon you'll look for a sugary snack to compensate. If you are making a sandwich without meat, cheese, or egg, look for a different way to pack up some protein. Beans, for instance in a bean dip, have protein, which you can add to your lunch as a dip with some veggies. Maybe you can toss some hard-boiled egg into a salad or add string cheese or a chunk of cheddar cheese as a snack. By and large I have not included a lot of onions, garlic, and scallions; even if you do brush your teeth after you eat, the smell sometimes lingers.

Tucking a few dark green lettuce leaves and some sprouts into any sandwich does not alter the taste significantly, but it will give you a few more vegetables every day, for which your body will thank you in the long run.

Try to make most of your sandwiches from whole, unadulterated foods with no preservatives, artificial dyes and flavors, MSG, etc. Choose turkey breast rather than salami (which contains all sorts of added chemicals), natural cheese instead of processed cheese, whole wheat and sprouted wheat bread rather than white bread, and all-fruit spread instead of jams and jellies with added sugar.

Making a lot of sandwiches is easier if you do it assembly-line style. Line up the slices of bread on the counter; spread them with butter, mayonnaise, or mustard; put the topping on; and top with remaining piece of bread. If you want to be really efficient, make extra sandwiches and freeze them. Look in the first section of this book for items that will and won't freeze well. If you are using soft bread, you can freeze the slices first so that they won't rip when you spread hard butter or peanut butter.

meatsandwiches

Most of the time, you'll end up making meat sandwiches. The way to keep them exciting is to vary the bread, the spread, the proteins, and the vegetable garnish. Portion control is key and your activity level and appetite will have to guide you. Limit the amount of processed meat products you eat; processed meats have all sorts of questionable additives and preservatives in them. Stick with roast beef, ham, and chicken or turkey breast, and go easy on salami and bologna sandwiches.

Try some of these winning combinations:

Sliced chicken breast, Swiss cheese, and caramelized onions

Sliced chicken breast, lettuce, tomato, and buttermilk dressing

Sliced chicken breast, shredded lettuce, shredded carrots, and peanut dressing

meatsandwiches

Sliced chicken breast, sliced apple, and mango chutney

Sliced chicken breast, provolone, Romaine lettuce, and Caesar salad

Sliced chicken breast, avocado, tomato, and salsa

Sliced turkey breast, lettuce, and cranberry sauce

Sliced turkey breast, lettuce, red pepper strips, and blue cheese dip

Sliced turkey breast, cheddar cheese, and ginger marmalade

Sliced turkey breast, roasted red pepper, pesto, and pine nuts

Sliced smoked turkey breast, sharp cheddar, roasted red peppers, and mayo-mustard spread

Sliced smoked turkey, avocado, tomatoes, and mayonnaise

Sliced roast beef, lettuce, tomato, bacon, and Russian dressing

Sliced roast beef, cheddar cheese, tomato, and mayonnaise

Sliced roast beef and oven-roasted vegetables

Sliced roast beef, sun-dried tomatoes, and buttermilk dressing

Sliced ham, lettuce, pineapple ring, and mayonnaise

Sliced ham, Swiss cheese, tomatoes, and buttermilk dressing

Sliced salami, pickles, and mustard

Sliced salami, provolone cheese, and caramelized onions

Lettuce Wraps

Wilted lettuce leaves make a great wrap. The only drawback is that you cannot very well make these in advance. Exact recipes don't work very well, because everything depends on the size of the leaves. So I will give you some suggestions and you can take it from there. Pack the lettuce leaves and the filling ingredients separately and don't forget the napkin.

> Whole Boston lettuce leaves
> Fillings, such as chopped grilled chicken, diced ham, grated
>   carrots, grated cucumbers, etc.
> Toppings, such as chopped peanuts or currants
> Dipping sauces, such as blue cheese dressing or soy sauce

To make the wraps, place a small amount of fillings and toppings in the center of the leaf. Fold over the bottom, then fold over the sides, and then fold the top flap. Dip the packet in the dipping sauce.

breadstotry

Good sandwich choices include whole wheat, rye, whole wheat bagels, focaccia, rice cakes, whole wheat crackers, whole grain wraps, whole grain waffles, whole wheat raisin bread, whole wheat cinnamon bread, flour tortillas. Less nutritious choices are white bread, hard rolls, hotdog rolls, croissants, graham crackers, and English muffins.

Keep breads in the freezer so they don't mold. Also, frozen bread doesn't tear when you apply a thick spread, such as stiff peanut butter or cold cream cheese.

Vegetable Square

This mild square contains four different kinds of vegetables, which makes it particularly healthy. I like using this as a "bread": I slice it in half and put a little cheese or flavored cream cheese in the middle.

MAKES 9–18 PIECES

1 6-ounce jar marinated artichokes
1 medium zucchini, grated (2 cups)
1 medium carrot, shredded
1 small onion, minced
2 eggs
⅓ cup feta cheese
¼ cup water
3 tablespoons marinade from marinated artichokes
1 cup whole wheat flour
2 teaspoons baking powder
1 teaspoon dried oregano

1. Preheat the oven to 375°F. Oil a 9-by-9-inch baking pan.

2. Drain the artichoke hearts, reserving the marinade. Chop the hearts and put them in a mixing bowl with the zucchini, carrot, and onion.

3. In a separate bowl combine the eggs, feta cheese, water, and 3 tablespoons of marinade. Mix well. Add to the vegetables and mix well.

4. Add the flour, baking powder, and oregano to the vegetable mixture and mix well.

5. Place the vegetable batter in the prepared baking pan, and smooth over the top a bit. Bake for 30 minutes. Cut into 9 squares; for a young child cut the squares into bars. Serve at room temperature.

Baked Sandwich

This is a good sandwich to make for yourself and a few lucky friends. At work heat the sandwiches briefly in a toaster oven or microwave.

SERVES 4

8 slices of whole wheat bread, buttered on one side
¼ cup grated Monterey Jack cheese
1 cup diced smoked turkey
¼ cup chopped red pepper
1 tablespoon chopped scallion
3 eggs, lightly beaten
2 cups low-fat milk

1. Preheat oven to 375°F.

2. In a 9-by-9-inch pan, place 4 slices of bread, buttered side down (trim the bread to fit). Sprinkle cheese, turkey, pepper, and scallion evenly over all. Top with the remaining slices of bread, buttered side up.

3. In a medium bowl, beat together eggs and milk. Pour the milk mixture over the sandwiches. Let sit for 15 minutes. Then bake the sandwiches for 40 minutes. Serve hot or let cool, wrap, and reheat for lunch.

BLT

Go ahead, have a BLT—but make it with some vegetarian and lower-in-fat substitutes. Smoked tempeh is a soybean product available at most supermarkets, much lower in fat than bacon. Be sure to get the smoked tempeh, as plain tempeh has very little flavor. You can also make this with a few bacon bits.

SERVES 1

2 slices bread, toasted if you like
Mayonnaise
2 lettuce leaves
½ tomato, sliced
4 smoked tempeh strips, or other bacon substitute

1. Spread the mayonnaise on the slices of bread. On one slice place a lettuce leaf, the tomato slices, and the tempeh. Top that with the other slice of lettuce and the remaining piece of bread.

2. Cut into triangles and wrap tightly in plastic wrap.

VARIATIONS: If you are a purist, by all means use bacon strips instead.

Try thinly sliced smoked tofu instead of the tempeh.

cheesesandwiches

Cheese sandwiches are an old standby but there is no reason to get bored. Try some different varieties from sharp cheeses, such as cheddar and blue cheese, to a mild cheese like goat cheese, and pair the cheese with a vegetable on the sandwich for some extra nutrition.

Mild cheddar cheese, tomato, lettuce, and mild mustard

Sharp cheddar cheese and pineapple preserves

Monterey Jack cheese, mushrooms, and green pepper sticks

Feta cheese, lettuce, tomato, and very thinly sliced red onion

Blue cheese, cucumber, and ginger marmalade

Mozzarella, roasted red pepper, pesto, and a sprinkle of dried basil

Gruyère, sun-dried tomato, and alfalfa sprouts

Gouda, anchovies, marinated red pepper, and chopped parsley

Smoked Gouda, chopped celery, and Caesar salad dressing

Thin slices of mozzarella, tomato slices, and a sprinkle of oregano

Ham and Cheese Sandwiches

A good combination of traditional all-American ingredients of ham and cheese, and a bunch of vegetables, which give you the nutrition that you need. By mashing the avocado with mustard you do not need mayonnaise and can save some calories.

MAKES 1 SANDWICH

½ avocado, sliced
1 teaspoon mustard
Salt
2 slices twelve-grain bread
1 slice ham
1 slice cheddar cheese
3 slices ripe tomato
Alfalfa sprouts

1. In a small bowl mash together the avocado, mustard, and salt.

2. Spread half of the avocado spread on each of the slices of bread. Layer the rest of the ingredients in order and put the second piece of bread on top. Wrap tightly in plastic wrap.

Egg Salad Sandwich

By making your own egg salad, you can control the amount of fat in it. And if you use organic eggs, you'll get superior nutrition. You can easily make this only with yogurt as a dressing, since the creamy texture comes in good part from the mashed egg yolks. Unless your doctor advises you to do so, don't omit the egg yolk, it won't taste as good and the yolk of a good quality egg provides many vital nutrients.

MAKES 1 SANDWICH

2 eggs, hard-boiled and peeled
1 teaspoon nonfat yogurt
1 teaspoon mayonnaise

Salt and pepper
2 lettuce leaves
2 slices of bread, toasted

1. Place the egg, yogurt, and mayonnaise in a bowl and mash thoroughly, mixing well. Add salt and pepper to taste.

2. Make the sandwich by placing a lettuce leaf on the bread, then the egg salad, then the second lettuce leaf, and the second piece of bread on top. Wrap tightly in plastic wrap.

eggsandwichideas

Hard-boiled eggs don't have to be used only for egg salad. Try one of these:

Sliced hard-boiled egg and mayonnaise with a little ground cumin or curry powder

Sliced hard boiled egg, lettuce, tomato, and equal mix of mayonnaise and ketchup

Sliced hard-boiled egg, romaine lettuce, tomato, anchovies, and mayonnaise

Sliced hard-boiled egg, pesto, and zucchini

Mashed Tofu Pockets

I thought of giving this sandwich a cute name, but it is better to face the issue head on: Tofu has a bad reputation, but in fact, it has a very neutral flavor. If you have not tried tofu, this might be the time! This recipe has a resemblance to egg salad, without the cholesterol. The turmeric is here to provide color, but scientists are finding that it provides healthful nutrients as well.

MAKES 2 SANDWICHES

8 ounces soft tofu
1 tablespoon mayonnaise
1 tablespoon low-fat yogurt
⅛ teaspoon turmeric
¼ cup minced fresh parsley
¼ teaspoon salt
Pinch pepper
Pinch paprika
Lettuce leaves
2 pita pockets, cut open

1. Mash together the tofu, mayonnaise, yogurt, and turmeric in a bowl until the salad has a uniform yellow color. Add the rest of the ingredients, except for lettuce, and mix well.

2. Line the pita pockets with lettuce leaves and fill them with the mashed tofu. Wrap tightly in plastic wrap.

Tahini, Honey, and Banana Sandwich

Tahini is made from sesame seeds, which are very high in calcium, so not only is this spread sweet and delicious, it packs a respectable nutritional punch as well.

MAKES 1 SANDWICH

1 to 2 tablespoons tahini
1 tablespoon honey
2 slices whole grain bread
Banana slices

Mix tahini and honey together. Spread mixture on the two slices of bread. Arrange banana slices on one piece of bread and top with the other piece of bread. (If you are making this sandwich at home and you want to be extra decadent, grill the banana sandwich lightly in butter.)

wrappingupyoursandwich

Instead of making "flat" sandwiches, try making wraps. It makes for an updated presentation, which is currently very popular. It also allows you to fold in some vegetables, which might otherwise be left out of a flat sandwich. Different breads for making wraps are available in the supermarket. You can also cut a pita bread in half horizontally, so that you have two flat rounds, which you can use for making small wraps. Always wrap this sandwich tightly in plastic wrap to keep the contents from falling out.

Tuna Fish Salad Sandwich

Although a tuna sandwich is one of the reliable old standbys, it does not have to be boring. That's why I like to add little bits of minced crunchy vegetables to my tuna salad. Line the slices of bread or the pita pocket with lettuce leaves so the bread does not get soggy. Choosing water-packed tuna over oil-packed will save you a lot of calories.

MAKES 1 SANDWICH

2 lettuce leaves

2 slices of bread or 1 pita pocket cut open on the top

3 ounces canned water-packed tuna, drained well

2 teaspoons mayonnaise

2 teaspoons low-fat yogurt

1 tablespoon minced celery

1 tablespoon minced carrot

Salt and pepper

1. Place clean and very dry lettuce leaves on the pieces of bread or in a pita pocket.

2. In a bowl mix the tuna, mayonnaise, and yogurt. Add the celery, carrot, salt, and pepper and mix again.

3. Place the salad on the lettuce leaves and put one slice of bread on the other, lettuce side down, or carefully scoop the salad into the pita pocket, inside the lettuce leaves. Wrap tightly in plastic wrap.

Salmon Salad Sandwich

This is the perfect lunch to make the day after you had poached salmon for dinner (see the recipe on page 152). Be sure to chill the salad right after you make it, and pack it cold into a lunchbox, adding a cold pack or frozen juice box for extra safety. You can also make the salad from scratch using canned salmon.

Salmon has beneficial omega-3 fats that we all need for healthy hearts and glowing skin, so if you like this, and your budget allows, try to serve it often.

MAKES 1 SANDWICH

1 cup poached salmon or canned salmon, drained
2 teaspoons nonfat yogurt
2 teaspoons mayonnaise
1 tablespoon poached scallions (optional)
Salt and pepper
2 slices whole wheat bread or 1 whole wheat pita pocket
   cut open at the top

1. Place the salmon, yogurt, mayonnaise, and scallions in a bowl and mix well. Add salt and pepper to taste. Chill.

2. Make a sandwich with the bread slices or fill the pita pocket. Wrap tightly in plastic wrap. Pack it very cold, and add an ice pack to the lunchbox.

Avocado and Sprouts Sandwich

This combination is not only delicious, it is also filled with many nutrients, because both avocadoes and sprouts have lots of vitamins and minerals. Be sure to give the avocado a sprinkle of lemon juice to keep it from discoloring to a disappointing, but perfectly edible, brown.

MAKES 1 SANDWICH

2 slices whole grain bread
Mayonnaise or Russian dressing (see page 103)
Avocado slices, sprinkled with lemon juice
Sprouts

Make a sandwich in the usual manner. Wrap tightly in plastic wrap.

VARIATIONS: Try blue cheese dressing or Caesar dressing.

Add additional vegetables, such as tomatoes, radishes, and cucumbers.

Add sliced egg, a slice of cheese, or a few anchovies.

Sushi Rolls

Sushi rolls, as made by well-trained Japanese chefs, are edible pieces of art. But you can make them even if you are not an artist; just adjust your expectations! There really is not much to it; if you can spread peanut butter on toast, you can make a nori roll good enough to eat (even if it is not pretty enough to display).

The special ingredients for sushi include nori sheets (thin black wraps made from seaweed), sushi rice (a special, sticky Japanese rice), tamari sauce (Japanese soy sauce), pickled ginger, and wasabi (a very hot mustard). These supplies might be found in your supermarket, but if not, you will be able to get them in your local health food store.

The idea is simple: You make sticky rice that you spread on a flat piece of nori. You pile on a few more ingredients, roll the thing up, and voilà, you have a sushi roll, more or less. For you bakers, think of how you'd make a jelly roll; the technique is the same. The only equipment you might need is a bamboo sushi mat. But in a pinch you can use a clean tea towel, and I have even rolled some with my hands. So go ahead; it's fun, healthy, and delicious.

If you have never seen this done, go on the Web where there are many sites with photographs that can give you the visual component that is missing here. But the best way to learn is to go to a sushi bar and watch a pro do it (what a great excuse to go!).

If you can't find sushi rice, you can use another rice (not instant or converted rice, which are designed to come out dry), cook it with some extra water, and let it rest in the pot after you take it off the heat.

Tamari sauce, wasabi, or pickled ginger are packed separately to be used as condiments.

MAKES 3 ROLLS

3 nori sheets
3 cups cooked sticky rice
3 tablespoons rice vinegar (do not substitute another vinegar)
1½ cups fillings

Filling options (notice nontraditional combinations, which look like dinner leftovers)

Avocado, cucumber, and carrots cut into julienne strips
Canned tuna, celery, zucchini
Imitation crabmeat or crabmeat, mayonnaise, avocado strips
Cooked salmon, cooked asparagus, little buttermilk dressing

1. Place a nori sheet on a bamboo sushi mat. Place a cup of cooked rice on the nori sheet and spread it out until it is evenly distributed, but leave 1 inch of nori sheet without rice.

2. Place the filling ingredients lengthwise down the center. Roll the sushi up as tightly as you can. Wet the last little bit of uncovered nori and close the seam. Cut into 1½-inch pieces with a sharp knife.

nut-butter sandwich ideas

There's no reason to limit yourself to the American standard of peanut butter and grape jelly. Many varieties of all-fruit spreads are available and make for some variation without adding lots of extra sugar. Spreading peanut butter instead of butter on your toast gives you a boost of protein and you avoid the saturated fat. Peanut and almond butter have mono-saturated fat instead. They're still high in calories, so use a light hand. And look in your supermarket for almond and cashew butters. They are delicious.

Peanut butter and all-fruit spread

Peanut butter and banana

Peanut butter, banana, and grated coconut

Peanut butter and pineapple slice

Peanut butter and apple butter

Peanut butter and raisins

Peanut butter and shredded coconut

Almond butter and all-fruit peach spread

Almond butter and apple slices

Almond butter and grated carrots

Cashew butter and all-fruit apricot spread

Cashew butter and pear slices

Cashew butter and dried cranberries

Pizza to Go Quesadilla Style

If you have a microwave at work you can heat these up. Or maybe you're one of the few adults who likes cold pizza.

SERVES 1 TO 2

2 flour tortillas
¼ cup tomato sauce or pizza sauce
¼ cup shredded cheddar cheese

1. Place one tortilla in the bottom of a nonstick skillet. Turn the heat on to low.

2. Spoon the tomato or pizza sauce on the tortilla and spread it out evenly. Sprinkle the cheese evenly over the sauce. Top with the second tortilla. Cook on both sides, like a grilled cheese sandwich.

3. Place the sandwich on a plate and let it cool. Cut it into wedges and wrap tightly in plastic wrap.

VARIATIONS: You can top the cheese with small quantities of vegetables, such as caramelized onions (see page 138), steamed broccoli and zucchini, and bits of meat, such as little pieces of smoked turkey and shredded cooked chicken.

Or make *Pizza to Go French-Bread Style:* Make a pizza out of French bread, which you've covered with pizza sauce topped with shredded cheese. Bake it in the oven until the cheese melts, cool it, and wrap it up. Or pack the sandwich before baking and heat it up in a microwave at work.

Calzones

The instructions for calzones have a "do this exactly" part and an improvisation part. The filling, size, and shape of these are completely up to you. I don't think I have ever made one that looked remotely as pretty as any of the illustrations I have seen, or any of the ones I have eaten in restaurants. I just happen to find pizza dough tough to work with, and you might, too. But that has not stopped me, and it shouldn't stop you either.

There are only two things you must pay attention to when making calzones: First, wet the seams of the dough before pressing them together; otherwise you will have an imperfect seal and your filling will melt and run out. Second, pizza dough must go into a hot oven if it is to come out right.

Calzones taste great hot out of the oven (though you want them to cool for a few minutes, since the filling will be very hot), but they are also good at room temperature the next day.

> 1 1-pound package frozen pizza dough, defrosted
> 2 to 4 cups fillings (recipes follow)
> 2 teaspoons vegetable oil

1. Preheat the oven to 450°F. This is not optional: you really must preheat the oven if you want your calzone to come out nice and crisp. Cover a baking sheet with aluminum foil.

2. Cut the dough into 6 pieces with a sharp, serrated knife. On a floured board roll out each of the pieces to a 6-inch circle.

3. Place a sixth of the filling in the center of the circle. Wet the edges of the dough with water and fold it over to make a half-moon shape. Pinch the edges carefully to seal them.

4. Brush the oil over the tops of the calzones and place them on the baking sheet. Place pan in the oven and turn the heat down to 375°F. Bake for about 25 minutes. Serve hot or at room temperature.

Calzone Fillings

1 cup shredded mozzarella

¾ cup marinara sauce

1 cup diced green pepper

3 cups Roasted Vegetables (recipe follows)

1 cup crumbled blue cheese or shredded cheddar cheese

4 ounces smoked turkey, sliced

2 cups chopped tomato

1 teaspoon dried oregano

1 cup shredded cheddar

1 cup Caramelized Onions (recipe follows)

1 cup shredded mozzarella

1 teaspoon dried oregano

Roasted Vegetables

Roasted vegetables are a great dinner dish, with a perfect lunch follow-up. Lots of variations are possible. If you do make this for dinner, you can also add some potatoes.

MAKES ABOUT 3 CUPS

1 small zucchini, cut into 1-inch chunks

1 carrot, cut into ½-inch slices

1 tomato, cut into 6 wedges

1 green pepper, cored and cut into ¾-inch chunks

1 medium onion, cut into ½-inch chunks

¼ cup olive oil

1 teaspoon salt

1½ teaspoons dried oregano

1½ teaspoons dried basil

1. Preheat oven to 375°F.

2. In a large bowl combine the zucchini, carrot, tomato, pepper, onion, and oil. Mix well with a large spoon so that all the vegetables are covered in oil. Sprinkle the salt, oregano, and basil over the vegetables and mix well again.

3. Place the vegetables and any leftover oil in a large roasting pan. Roast the vegetables for 50 minutes, turning occasionally, or until they are browned and feel soft when pierced with a fork.

4. Once the vegetables have cooled, store them in the refrigerator in an airtight container.

Caramelized Onions

Heaping a few caramelized onions on a sandwich pumps up the meal from just OK to fabulous. Because of the long, slow cooking, the onions lose all their bite and become naturally sweet and mellow. These keep for a week or so in the refrigerator, so make as much as you think you can use in that time period. Serve on sandwiches hot or at room temperature.

MAKES ½ CUP

1 onion, thinly sliced
1 tablespoon olive oil
½ teaspoon tamari or soy sauce

In a large frying pan, heat the oil. Add the onion slices. Over low to medium heat, very slowly brown the onions, about 10 to 15 minutes. Add the tamari or soy sauce and mix. Cool and refrigerate.

VARIATION: *Barbecued Onions:* For some extra taste zing, add 1 or 2 teaspoons of bottled barbecue sauce in the last few minutes.

Quesadillas

Quesadillas are usually served as appetizers, but with a substantial filling can easily become a light lunch. It is really nothing more than the Mexican version of our grilled cheese sandwich, except you use flour tortillas instead of bread. Make them at home and reheat them briefly in a microwave at work. Try one of the variations on the next page when you want something different.

MAKES 1 QUESADILLA OR 4 WEDGES

2 tablespoons refried beans

1 tablespoon diced green chiles

¼ teaspoon ground cumin

2 flour tortillas

2 tablespoons grated Monterey Jack cheese

½ tomato, chopped

¼ cup corn kernels (fresh or frozen and thawed)

1 teaspoon minced fresh cilantro

1. Mix the beans, chiles, and cumin in a small bowl.

2. Place one flour tortilla on the counter and spread it with the bean mix. Sprinkle the remaining ingredients over the beans in the order given: cheese, tomato, corn, and cilantro. Top with the remaining tortilla.

3. Cook the quesadilla over medium heat in a large, nonstick skillet until the cheese is melted.

4. Cut into 4 wedges and eat the hot quesadilla immediately, or let it cool. Wrap tightly and refrigerate. Heat slightly in the microwave before eating.

VARIATIONS: Your imagination is your only obstacle here. The next time you are in an upscale pizza parlor, look at the combinations they have created for their exotic pizzas and see if you can glean some inspiration from them. The only requirements are melted cheese to hold the quesadilla together, and that the combined flavors of your ingredients contrast nicely but do not clash.

Try other cheeses—feta, blue cheese, or cheddar.

Add small quantities of chopped leftover meat, some grilled chicken, smoked salmon, or crumbled, cooked sausage.

Add lots of other vegetables such as spinach, red or green peppers, and marinated artichoke hearts.

Try spreading a little mango chutney, cranberry preserves, or dill mustard for an unusual burst of flavor.

goatcheesesandwiches

Goat cheese is available from mild to pungent. If you are not familiar with it, try some of the softer milder varieties and work your way up. I love the taste and the following unusual sandwich suggestions should get you started:

Goat cheese and roasted vegetables on peasant bread

Goat cheese, chopped walnuts, honey, and sprinkle of thyme on a baguette

Goat cheese, roasted red peppers, diced black olives on twelve-grain bread

Dinner to Lunch

he real trick to making nutritious, fast lunches is planning ahead. Making a dinner that automatically supplies you with a lunch or two is a good way to do that. To some extent the idea here is that if you more or less cook for an army at home, you can eat like a king on the road. No one would make a pan of lasagna just for one lunch, but reheated lasagna at lunchtime is a luxurious treat.

The other timesaver is to make lunch the night before. You are cleaning up the kitchen anyway; just tack on 5 more minutes of work and lunch is done. Chop up the last two stalks of leftover steamed broccoli, the three leftover pieces of lettuce, that half tomato, and that last stalk of celery; take the last slice of roast beef and cut it into little cubes; add a cup of leftover macaroni from yesterday; add a little dressing and mix; top with a little feta cheese to make it fabulous; and voilà: it's lunch for tomorrow. Think of how many ways you save here: instead of throwing away the last little bits of dinner, you are using them to make lunch, so your ingredients are practically free. You don't have to think about lunch in the morning, so you make your morning routine less hectic. And you don't have to go out and stand in line during a busy lunch hour: you can eat your nutritious lunch in peace and maybe take the time you save and go for a walk!

Garlic Roasted Chicken

If your oven has the space, never make less than two of these for dinner, because it is mighty handy to have leftover roast chicken on hand to make chicken salad with.

Don't let chicken stand around at room temperature too long after the meal; process the chicken right away into the next meal or place it in the refrigerator.

SERVES 4 TO 6

1 4-pound roasting chicken, fully defrosted if previously frozen
5 whole garlic cloves, peeled, crushed, and cut in quarters
1 lemon
1 teaspoon dried thyme
Salt and pepper to taste
1 cup coarsely chopped onions
1 teaspoon olive oil

1. Preheat the oven to 350°F. Place a rack in a roasting pan. Remove the giblets from the cavity of the chicken and set aside for roasting separately.

2. Wash the chicken thoroughly with water. Dry it with paper towels and place it, breast side up, on the rack set into the roasting pan. Pour enough water into the pan to cover the bottom.

3. Place the garlic cloves in the cavity. Wash the whole lemon thoroughly and cut off a third of it (reserve the rest of the lemon for another use). Squeeze some of the lemon juice over the chicken and place the lemon, peel and all, into the cavity.

4. Sprinkle thyme, salt, and pepper into the cavity and over the chicken. Tuck the wings close to the breast.

5. Place the chicken into the oven and bake until done. If the top the chicken browns too quickly, place a loose aluminum foil tent over the breast.

6. Wash and dry the giblets. In a bowl combine them with the onions and oil. Put the mixture in a small ovenproof dish and roast it alongside the chicken for 30 minutes or until the onions start to brown. Remove from oven and cool. Refrigerate until you are ready to make chicken stock or soup.

Honey-Mustard Chicken

Make this very flavorful chicken for dinner but be sure to save some for lunch in a chicken salad, sliced thinly in a sandwich, or on top of a Caesar salad. If you want to make this dish with a quartered chicken, just look in an all-purpose cookbook to adjust the cooking times.

SERVES 4 FOR DINNER; 2 MORE FOR LUNCH

¼ cup honey
¼ cup Dijon mustard
1 teaspoon dried basil
6 skinless bone-in chicken breasts

1. Preheat oven to 350°F. Line a baking dish with aluminum foil (for easy clean-up).

2. In a small bowl combine the honey, mustard, and basil. Brush the sauce all over the breasts, and place them in the prepared pan.

3. Bake the chicken for 30 minutes or until they are cooked through. Serve hot for dinner.

4. Cool the leftovers, cover, and refrigerate.

Raspberry and Peach Chicken Salad

In the summertime I use the oven early in the morning, when the house is still cool. So roast a chicken in the morning and you'll have plenty to make this salad and other chicken dishes with. This salad also works well with grilled chicken, so grill some extra pieces for dinner and set them aside. If you are making this salad for a special lunch party, garnish with edible flowers such as pansies and nasturtium blossoms.

SERVES 4

2 cups diced roasted chicken
1 cup diced fresh peaches
¾ cup fresh raspberries
8 cups mixed salad greens
¼ cup chopped pecans
½ teaspoon minced fresh oregano
Fruit Salad Dressing (see page 68)

1. Gently mix the chicken, peaches, and berries in a large bowl.

2. Line each of 4 plates with 2 cups of the mixed greens. Place the chicken salad on top.

3. In a small bowl mix the pecans and the oregano. Sprinkle the pecan mix over the salad and greens.

4. To take it with you for lunch, place the greens at the bottom of a plastic bowl, place the chicken salad on top, and sprinkle the pecan mixture over all. Pack the dressing separately and pour over the salad just before eating.

Crispy Oven-Baked Chicken

Marinating chicken in buttermilk or yogurt is a fabulous way to tenderize it. It is the secret behind the tenderness of Tandoori Chicken, a necessary trick in a country where chickens were not bred for tenderness. This is great at room temperature, but if you want to eat it warm, heat it up briefly in a microwave.

MAKES 6 PIECES

1 cup buttermilk, or ½ cup plain yogurt mixed with ½ cup water

1½ teaspoons dried oregano

1 teaspoon dried basil

½ teaspoon dried thyme

2 (1-pound) chicken breasts, bone-in, each cut into thirds

1 to 2 cups seasoned breadcrumbs

Salt and pepper to taste (optional)

1. In a large bowl combine the buttermilk or yogurt and water mixture, oregano, basil, and thyme. Add the pieces of chicken and cover. Marinate for 2 to 4 hours, turning the pieces once in a while.

2. Preheat the oven to 350°F.

3. Place the breadcrumbs in a shallow bowl. One piece at a time, take the chicken out of the marinade and roll it in the breadcrumbs, covering the piece completely. Place the pieces meat-side up in a baking dish.

4. Bake the chicken for 40 minutes or until done. Serve immediately, or cool and serve at room temperature.

Curried Chicken Salad

Leftover Honey-Mustard Chicken (see page 143) makes a great beginning to this curried chicken and pasta salad. If you served the chicken with pasta and peas at night, you'll have all the makings of this terrific salad. Mix in additional vegetables, such as grated carrots, if you like, to be closer to getting your full daily quota of vegetables. Serve this on dark bread for a sandwich or on a plate with pita bread on the side.

SERVES 3 FOR LUNCH

2 Honey-Mustard Chicken breasts, fully cooked, cut up
1 cup cooked medium pasta shells
1 cup peas, cooked
1 apple, cored and diced
2 medium stalks celery, chopped
1 green onion, equal parts white and green, minced
⅓ cup low-fat yogurt
2 tablespoons mayonnaise
1 teaspoon curry powder
¼ teaspoon ground cumin

1. In a large bowl gently mix the chicken, pasta, peas, apple, celery, and onion.

2. In a separate small bowl, mix the yogurt, mayonnaise, curry, and cumin. Pour over the chicken and pasta mixture and combine gently but thoroughly. Cover and refrigerate until serving time.

Barbecued Pot Roast

Giving your pot roast a barbecue flavor will not only provide an extra boost for your dinner, it will also give you a terrific piece of meat to make a sandwich from. You might want to reserve a portion for sandwiches for the next day before you serve it up; otherwise, it just might disappear at the dinner table!

SERVES 4

4 pounds pot roast
½ teaspoon olive oil
1½ cups tomato sauce
1½ tablespoons Worcestershire sauce
1 tablespoon lemon juice
1 teaspoon light brown sugar
1 cup finely chopped onions
8 carrots, scraped and cut into 1-inch sections
4 medium potatoes, scrubbed and cut into 1½-inch chunks
4 celery stalks, washed and cut into 1-inch sections

1. Preheat the oven to 350°F.

2. Heat the olive oil in a Dutch oven or large frying pan. Add the roast and brown it on all sides. Place the roast in a roasting pan.

3. In a separate bowl mix the tomato sauce, Worcestershire sauce, lemon juice, and brown sugar. Pour the sauce over the meat. Sprinkle the onions over all. Arrange the vegetables around the beef. Cover tightly with aluminum foil and place in oven. Bake for 2½ hours or until the vegetables are done and the beef is tender.

4. Have the pot roast and vegetables for dinner and reserve the left-over meat for sandwiches for lunch.

Chili

I have been told that adding beans is not really authentic, but they are a great source of nutrients, so it is a good idea anyway. Adjust the amount of chili powder depending on how hot you like it. A corn muffin and a green salad give you a balanced and delicious lunch.

SERVES 4 TO 6

1½ tablespoons olive oil
1 medium onion, chopped
1 green pepper, chopped
1 clove garlic, minced
1 pound ground beef
2 tablespoons chili powder (or more to taste)
1½ teaspoons cumin powder
1½ teaspoons dried oregano
2 cups spaghetti sauce
1 16-ounce can kidney beans

1. In a large frying pan, heat the olive oil and sauté the onions and peppers on medium heat until the onions are transparent. Clear a space in the middle of the pan and add the garlic. Sauté the garlic for 20 seconds. Transfer the mixture to a large pot.

2. In the same pan brown the ground beef, breaking it up with the back of a spoon. Add a little more olive oil if you need it (it will depend on how lean the ground beef is). When the beef is browned, pour off the fat and add the beef to the pot with the onion mixture.

3. Add the rest of the ingredients and bring to a simmer. Simmer the chili for 20 minutes. Serve hot.

4. For lunch pack some chili, reheated, in a thermos. You can also freeze leftovers for future use.

Meatloaf

This is a simple, foolproof recipe. The food processor technique allows you to get the meatloaf into the oven in a matter of minutes. The advantage of baking meatloaf in a nontraditional brownie pan is that you automatically have flat pieces of meatloaf that will fit perfectly on a piece of bread for a sandwich. This recipe is easily doubled (bake it in a loaf pan, for 1 hour). If you are well organized, make an extra one and freeze it, for the next meal.

SERVES 4 TO 6

2 slices bread
1 egg
¼ cup ketchup
1 teaspoon Worcestershire sauce
1 teaspoon dried oregano
1 pound ground beef

1. Preheat the oven to 350°F.

2. Put the bread slices in a food processor fitted with the steel blade. Process until they turn into fine crumbs.

3. Add the egg, ketchup, Worcestershire sauce, and oregano and process until well blended.

4. Add the ground beef and process until all is well blended.

5. Put the beef mixture into a 9-inch-square baking pan and smooth it out. Bake for 30 minutes. Serve hot for dinner or at room temperature in a sandwich.

Beef Stew

A heavy stew will warm and nourish you when the winter winds are howling. It freezes well and heats up perfectly in a microwave at lunchtime.

The secret of a good stew is browning the meat cubes a few at a time. This is the step most people skimp on, and it ruins the stew beyond hope from the start. Here's why: The moment the cold cubes hit the pan, the pan cools down. If too much meat is browned at the same time, the pan cools down so much that none of the meat really sears, and this is the process that seals flavor inside the meat. So be patient, take your time browning the beef, and be rewarded with a fabulous stew.

SERVES 4

1 to 1½ pounds beef stew meat, cut in 1-inch cubes

1 tablespoon whole wheat flour

½ teaspoon salt

Pepper

½ teaspoon dried thyme

½ teaspoon dried basil

1 tablespoon oil

1 cup chopped onions

1 cup red wine

1 cup water

1½ teaspoons Worcestershire sauce

2 celery stalks, cut up in 1-inch chunks (1½ cups)

2 carrots, cut up in medallions (1½ cups)

1 sweet potato, cut up in 1-inch cubes (2 cups)

1. Put the stew meat in a bowl. Sprinkle the flour, salt, pepper, thyme, and basil over all, and mix well.

2. In a frying pan, heat the oil and brown the meat a few cubes at a time. As the pieces of beef brown, transfer them to a large stove-top casserole.

3. In the same frying pan, fry the onions until they are translucent and starting to brown. Add the onions to the meat in the casserole.

4. Pour the wine, water, and Worcestershire sauce into the frying pan and bring to a boil, scraping the brown pieces from the bottom. Pour the liquid into the casserole. Mix well.

5. Bring the meat mixture to a boil, cover, and turn down the heat. Simmer on low heat for $1\frac{1}{2}$ hours.

6. Add the celery, carrots, and potato. Cover and simmer for 1 hour, stirring occasionally (the vegetables might sit on top of the liquid, but will steam to perfection). Serve hot or freeze and reheat. Use leftover stew for lunch. Reheat and spoon into a wide-mouthed thermos for lunch.

VARIATIONS: Substitute white potatoes for the sweet potatoes.

Substitute other vegetables for the celery and carrots, such as fennel, turnip, or green pepper.

Poached Salmon

Easy, fast, delicious, healthy, and leftovers make a great lunch salad. Salmon's omega-3 fatty acids are a necessary nutrient for us all, and will make for beautiful, healthy-looking skin—surely the best press you could give a food.

SERVES 4

1½ teaspoons olive oil
3 scallions, white and 3 inches of green, minced
1 cup white wine
1½ pounds salmon fillet
Salt and pepper
1 tablespoon sour cream
1 tablespoon snipped fresh dill

1. Heat the oil briefly in a frying pan. Add the scallions and fry them for a minute.

2. Add the salmon and wine and sprinkle with salt and pepper. Heat the wine slowly, but do not let it come to a boil. Cover the pan.

3. Simmer just below boiling until the salmon is cooked through (this will depend entirely on how thick the fillet is).

4. Remove the salmon to a warm serving plate. Add the sour cream to the poaching liquid, heat through without letting it come to a boil, and pour over the salmon. Sprinkle dill on top.

5. Serve with steamed red potatoes and baby carrots. Leftover salmon can be used to make Salmon Salad Sandwich (see page 130).

Salmon Tortellini Salad

Salmon is so mild tasting that you need to be careful not to over-whelm the flavor when you mix it with other ingredients. Cheese-filled tortellini give this salad a rich flavor, but you can make the salad with any cooked pasta.

SERVES 2 FOR LUNCH

1 cup leftover poached salmon, flaked

1 cup cooked tortellini

1 carrot, shredded

1 zucchini, shredded

¼ cup reduced-fat sour cream

1 tablespoon minced fresh dill

½ teaspoon Worcestershire sauce

1 tablespoon grated Parmesan cheese

1. In a large bowl mix the salmon, tortellini, carrots, and zucchini. In a separate small bowl, thoroughly mix the sour cream, dill, and Worcestershire sauce. Pour the sour cream dressing over the salmon and mix thoroughly but gently.

2. Sprinkle the Parmesan on top. Refrigerate until serving time.

Stuffed Baked Potatoes

A stuffed potato is a meal in itself. Just bake a few extra potatoes when you make dinner, and stuff them when you are cleaning up. At work, you just need to warm them through.

MAKES 2 POTATOES

2 large baked potatoes
2 tablespoons milk
2 tablespoons grated cheddar
1 teaspoon bacon bits
Salt and pepper to taste

1. Cut a slice from the top of the potatoes. Scoop the pulp out and place in a bowl.

2. Mash the potato pulp, milk, cheese, bacon bits, salt, and pepper. Refill the potato shells.

3. Wrap each potato in plastic wrap. For lunch heat in microwave until hot.

VARIATIONS: *Tuna Potatoes:* Add 4 tablespoons of canned drained tuna fish to the potato pulp and omit the bacon bits.

Vegetable Potatoes: Add a few tablespoons of cooked vegetables such as chopped broccoli or chopped carrots.

Chive Potatoes: Add 2 tablespoons of minced chives to the pulp.

Vegetarian Casserole

This casserole makes a splendid dinner and is very good to take to the office the next day. Just warm it up and serve with a crusty piece of bread.

1 cup chopped onions
2 tablespoons olive oil
¾ cup chopped green pepper
¾ cup chopped red pepper
4 carrots, chopped
½ small head green cabbage, chopped
2 cups vegetable broth
2 tablespoons tomato paste
½ teaspoon dried oregano
½ teaspoon dried basil
Tabasco sauce
2 teaspoons apple cider vinegar
1 10-ounce package frozen peas
Salt and pepper

1. In a large pan, sauté the onions in olive oil until they are translucent. Add the peppers and sauté 5 minutes more. Add the carrots, cabbage, broth, tomato paste, oregano, basil, a few shakes of Tabasco, and vinegar. Bring to a boil, reduce the heat, cover, and let simmer for 25 minutes.

2. Stir in the frozen peas and cook through for 5 minutes, or until they are done. Add salt and pepper to taste.

3. For lunch, package in a microwave-safe container and reheat until hot.

Double Shortcut Lasagna

I love this lasagna for its two timesaving shortcuts. First, you don't have to cook the noodles separately; they cook while the lasagna bakes. The second shortcut is to chop the onion, celery, and garlic in the food processor.

I like my lasagna without meat, but feel free to add a pound of cooked ground beef to the tomato sauce.

Since lasagna freezes so well, make two and give yourself an easy meal some other time.

MAKES 15 PIECES

1 26-ounce jar pasta sauce

1 cup water

1 cup red wine

1 onion, peeled and cut in large chunks

1 stalk celery, cut in large chunks

3 cloves garlic, quartered

1½ teaspoons dried oregano

1 pound part-skim mozzarella

2 eggs

1 10-ounce package frozen spinach, cooked according
   to package directions, squeezed dry

3 cups part-skim ricotta cheese

Salt and pepper to taste

½ cup grated Parmesan

1 pound uncooked lasagna noodles

1. Preheat the oven to 350°F. Take out a 9-by-13-inch baking dish.

2. In a large mixing bowl, combine the pasta sauce, water, and wine and mix well. Set aside.

3. In a food processor fitted with a steel blade, combine a cup of the tomato and wine sauce with the onion, celery, garlic, and oregano. Pulse the processor on and off, scraping down the sides a few times, until the vegetables are in uniform little pieces. Do not process until all the vegetables are liquefied. Add the vegetable mixture to the rest of the tomato and wine mixture and blend well.

4. Change the blade in the processor to a coarse grind and grate the mozzarella. Set the mozzarella aside in a bowl.

5. In a large bowl beat the eggs well. Add the spinach and ricotta and mix well. Season with salt and pepper if desired.

6. In assembling the lasagna, the only trick is to distribute the ingredients evenly over the entire surface. Pour a cup of the sauce in the bottom of the baking dish. On top of that place a layer of uncooked lasagna noodles. Pour a cup of the sauce over the noodles, then a third of the ricotta mix, then a third of the mozzarella. Repeat this twice more: noodles, sauce, ricotta, and mozzarella.

7. Finish with a final layer of noodles and pour the remaining sauce evenly over all. Sprinkle the top with Parmesan cheese. The lasagna should not reach to the top of the pan because the noodles will expand a bit as they cook.

8. Cover the pan tightly with aluminum foil and bake for 1 hour.

9. Remove the foil and continue baking, uncovered, for 15 minutes, or until the noodles are soft in the center (a knife should go in easily).

10. Let the lasagna rest for 10 minutes before serving.

11. Freeze leftover portions in serving sizes. For lunch, pack a serving in a microwave-proof container. Heat in the microwave until hot.

Corn Cheese Pie

This is a corn-filled quiche, delicious at every temperature. Bring along a green salad with a vinaigrette dressing and you have a delicious and well-balanced meal.

MAKES 1 PIE

1 ready-made 9-inch pie shell

20 ounces canned kernel corn

1 cup grated sharp cheddar cheese

3 scallions, equal parts green and white, minced

4 eggs

1½ cups low-fat milk

½ teaspoon dried oregano

½ teaspoon dried thyme

½ teaspoon salt

¼ teaspoon freshly ground pepper

1. Preheat the oven to 350°F.

2. Sprinkle the corn, cheese, and scallions into the pie shell.

3. In a bowl beat together the eggs, milk, oregano, thyme, salt, and pepper. Pour it over the corn.

4. Bake the pie for 35 minutes or until it is firm and slightly brown.

5. Eat warm, or cool, slice, wrap, and bring for lunch. Eat cold or warm slightly in a toaster oven or microwave.

Crustless Broccoli Quiche

This quiche reheats very well in the microwave and with a large green salad and some grapes for dessert makes a wonderfully indulgent lunch. Though there is a fair amount of dairy in this dish, the absence of a pastry crust makes its calorie count a lot lower than a commercial quiche.

MAKES 1 QUICHE

4 thick slices turkey ham or fully cooked ham, cubed
3 bacon strips, cut into ½-inch lengths
½ pound fresh mushrooms, sliced
1 cup chopped broccoli florets
1 cup low-fat milk
1 cup half-and-half
4 eggs
½ cup all-purpose flour
1 cup shredded mild cheddar cheese
¼ teaspoon salt
Pepper to taste

1. Preheat the oven to 450°F. Grease a 9-inch tart pan.

2. Over medium heat sauté the turkey ham and bacon until the bacon gives up its fat. Add the mushrooms and sauté until the liquid is released from the mushrooms. Add the broccoli and steam the broccoli in the mushroom liquid until the broccoli is bright green and most of the mushroom liquid is evaporated.

3. In a large bowl mix the milk, half-and-half, eggs, and flour until very well mixed. You can use a blender if you wish. Add the cheese, salt, and pepper. Add the ham mixture to the milk mixture, stir briefly, and pour into the prepared tart pan.

4. Bake the quiche for 45 minutes or until done. Serve hot or warm.

Fruits

Not only are fruits delicious, they are good for you besides. They are perfect additions to your bagged lunch, and you may also want to take extra fruit for morning and afternoon snacks.

Wash all fruit, even the fruit you intend to peel. Fruits, especially those that are imported from abroad, are sprayed with all sorts of nasty stuff to keep even nastier stuff from entering the country and our food supply. The outside of the fruit can easily contain some left-over residue, and your best bet is to wash it off.

When fresh fruit isn't available or feasible, take dried fruit. Good quality fruit leathers are made of 100 percent fruit, so they are a good, sweet snack, and very easy to carry for lunch. In addition, dried fruits are great additions to gorp and granola.

Fruit Packing and Salad Making

Be sure to pack fresh fruits in crushproof and leakproof containers. Some fruit, such as bananas and mandarin oranges, come perfectly packaged in their own biodegradable shells.

Because of their delicate nature, fresh fruit salads intended for lunch are often best made in the morning; this way they retain much of their good looks and great nutrients. The reason is this: Many fruits are healthy for us because of their vitamin C content. However, vitamin C is very susceptible to oxidation; in other words, it starts to break down the moment it starts to come into contact with oxygen. So don't make your fruit salad or fruit cup too far in advance and you'll get maximum benefit.

You might want to chill the fruit and place it in a chilled thermos; fruit will stay fresh longer that way.

Apples

Apples turn brown when they are exposed to air. Of all the apple varieties, Cortlands keep from turning dark longer than other varieties. There are a couple of solutions to this general problem:

Wash the apple, cut it into slices, and dip the slices in (diluted) lemon juice; or wash it, quarter and core it, and reassemble the pieces. Wrap tightly in plastic wrap.

For a real treat, wash the apple and core it (a melon ball scooper works well) while keeping the apple whole (as if you were going to make baked apples). Stuff the apple with almond butter. Cap it off with raisins.

Dried apples are chewy and soft.

Apples are high in dietary fiber and contribute vitamin C.

Selma's Apple Salad

This is a classic combination; my mother used to make me the baby version of this salad when I was a child. She shredded an apple, mixed it with a mashed banana, and poured the freshly squeezed juice of one orange over all. Delicious.

MAKES 1 CUP

½ apple, chopped
½ banana, sliced
1 tablespoon lemon juice
1 tablespoon water
½ orange, peeled, in sections, each section cut in thirds

Toss the apple and banana gently in the lemon juice, which has been diluted with the tablespoon of water. Add the orange and mix gently.

Apricots

A great way to bring this delicate fruit to work is to cut it in half, remove the pit, and reassemble it. Wrap it tightly in plastic wrap.

Dried apricots are either treated with sulfites to retain their orange color, or are naturally dried and look more brown and leathery. I prefer the latter. To cook with dried apricots, plump them in hot water for 30 minutes, and dry them off before you use them.

Dried or fresh apricots are high in vitamins A and C.

Apricot Mango Salad

MAKES 1 CUP

1 apricot, chopped

½ cup diced mango

2 tablespoons slivered almonds

2 tablespoons orange juice

Gently mix the apricot, mango, almonds, and juice.

Bananas

Bananas are handy to take for lunch because they are so easy to peel, but they need extra protection.

If your bananas are getting too ripe to eat, peel them and freeze them in chunks in plastic bags. They are great to have on hand for banana bread and for putting in milkshakes and smoothies. They will turn dark when they are frozen, but that will make no difference to the final result. For a fast, healthy ice cream, take some partly defrosted bananas and some all-fruit spread and process them in a food processor with a steel blade until you have frozen banana mush. Eat it right away.

Dried bananas end up like hard chips (as opposed to most other dried fruits, which are still soft and pliable when dry).

Bananas are a good source of fiber, vitamin C, and potassium.

Banana Jicama Salad

MAKES 1 CUP

1 small banana, cut into chunks
½ cup chopped jicama
1 tablespoon chopped peanuts
1 teaspoon honey
1 teaspoon unsweetened grated coconut

Gently mix the banana and jicama. Sprinkle the peanuts on top. Drizzle the honey over all and sprinkle with coconut.

Berries

Berries are a good source of vitamin C. They are great to add to fruit salads and yogurt, but they will stain your clothes, fingers, and teeth.

Triple Berry Salad

MAKES 1 CUP

½ cup sliced fresh strawberries

¼ cup blueberries

¼ cup raspberries

¼ cup low-fat plain yogurt

Gently mix together the ingredients.

Cherries

Cherries have pits, so you need to make a decision whether to pit them beforehand, which will make them leak juice, or do it at your desk if you can get rid of the pit discreetly enough.

Dried cherries are delicious but expensive, and not all of them have the pits removed, so be aware of what you are buying.

Cherries are a good source of vitamin C and fiber.

Cherry Cantaloupe Salad

MAKES 1½ CUPS

¾ cup pitted cherries

¾ cup cantaloupe (scooped out with a melon scooper)

¼ cup reduced-fat sour cream

1 tablespoon toasted pine nuts

Gently mix the cherries, cantaloupe, and sour cream. Sprinkle with the pine nuts.

Cranberries

Fresh cranberries are too tart to eat fresh most of the time. This salad, however, combines that tartness with sweetness and works very well. Try the (sugared) dried varieties as a snack.

Cranberries are a good source of vitamin C.

Cranberry Citrus Salad

MAKES 1 CUP

½ orange, peeled, in sections, sections cut into thirds

¼ grapefruit, peeled, in sections, sections cut into fourths

¼ cup chopped fresh cranberries

2 tablespoons unsweetened shredded coconut

2 tablespoons grape juice

Gently mix together all the ingredients.

Dates and Figs

Dried dates and figs make a delicious snack. They are naturally very sweet because they are high in natural sugar. They are also good sources of fiber. Fresh figs are delicious, but bruise and spoil easily, so eat them soon after you get them home.

Figs and Goat Cheese

SERVES 4

4 fresh figs

4 tablespoons mild goat cheese

Cut the figs in half, spread some goat cheese over the cut side, and get ready to swoon.

Grapefruit

Depending on the variety, grapefruits can be bitter or sweet, so find the type you like and remember its name.

Grapefruit is high in vitamin C and is a good source of vitamin A.

Grapefruit Ambrosia Salad

MAKES 1 $^1/_2$ CUPS

½ grapefruit, peeled, cut into sections, sections cut into fourths

½ orange, peeled, cut into sections, cut into thirds

½ cup pineapple pieces

¼ cup shredded unsweetened coconut

¼ cup nonfat yogurt

Gently mix the grapefruit, orange, pineapple, and coconut with the yogurt.

Grapes and Raisins

A few clusters of grapes make a convenient snack. If you dislike pits, make sure you are buying the seedless grape varieties, but that will limit your options. You'll miss a lot by not trying all the different varieties of grapes.

Raisins are a sweet snack to put in a lunchbag, and a supply of them in little boxes is good to have on hand.

Grapes are high in vitamin C. Raisins provide a fair amount of potassium.

Grape Chicken Salad

MAKES 1 1/4 CUPS

1/2 cup halved seedless grapes

1/2 cup chopped cooked chicken breast

1/2 cup chopped endive

1 teaspoon minced fresh basil leaves

1 tablespoon yogurt

Salt and pepper to taste

Gently mix the grapes, chicken breast, endives, basil, and yogurt. Season with salt and pepper to taste.

Kiwi

If you want to take a kiwi to work, you can cut it in half, reassemble it, and wrap it snugly in plastic wrap. The soft flesh can then be scooped out with a spoon.

Kiwifruit are high in vitamin C and are a good source of fiber and potassium.

Kiwi Salad

MAKES 1 CUP

2 kiwi, peeled and diced
2 Brazil nuts, chopped
¼ cup vanilla yogurt
Sprinkle of ground nutmeg

Gently mix kiwi, yogurt, and nuts. Sprinkle with nutmeg.

Mangoes and Papaya

Mangoes are probably my favorite fruit, but they are not the easiest to eat. For a bag lunch, this fruit will work only if you peel it and cut the flesh into little pieces in advance. Mango is high in vitamin A and is a good source of vitamin C.

Papayas can be peeled and seeded and cut into chunks for salad, or cut in half, seeded, and wrapped in plastic wrap. The soft papaya flesh can then be scooped out of the skin with a spoon. It is high in vitamin C and a good source of fiber and folate.

Tropical Fruit Salad

MAKES 1 CUP

½ papaya, seeded and diced

½ cup diced mango

¼ cup chopped shelled hazelnuts

¼ cup unsweetened yogurt

1 tablespoon granola

Gently mix the papaya, mango, hazelnuts, and yogurt. Sprinkle granola over all.

Melons

Cantaloupe, muskmelon, and honeydew are juicy and perfect when served in slices or in fruit salad.

Watermelon has lots of seeds (except for the seedless variety). For those young at heart, having a seed-spitting contest might be an excellent stress reliever at lunch, though I am sure your entire company will be grateful if you take that contest outside!

Cantaloupes are high in vitamins C and A and are a good source of potassium and folate. Honeydew melon is high in vitamin C. Watermelon is high in vitamins C and A.

Triple Melon Salad

MAKES 2 CUPS

¾ cup cantaloupe chunks

¾ cup honeydew chunks

¾ cup seeded watermelon chunks

¼ cup orange juice

Gently mix cantaloupe, honeydew, and watermelon chunks. Pour orange juice over all.

Oranges, Tangerines, and Mandarins

Thick-skinned oranges can be scored deeply and then can be peeled easily at work. Mandarin oranges are perfect to bring along in a bag lunch, because they peel so easily.

Cut sections of all citrus fruits are perfect in a fruit salad.

All citrus is high in vitamin C.

Orange and Cilantro Salad

MAKES 1 CUP

1 orange, peeled, cut into sections, then in thirds

¼ cup dried cranberries

1 teaspoon minced fresh cilantro

1 teaspoon lemon juice

1 teaspoon coconut oil

Gently mix the orange, cranberries, and cilantro. Sprinkle lemon juice and oil over all. Mix again.

Peaches and Nectarines

To make a peach or nectarine easier to eat at work, you can cut it in half at home, remove the pit, and reassemble the halves. If you don't like the fuzzy skin of a peach, you'll definitely want to peel it at home, because it is a slippery and juicy job, not suitable for the office. Or make a fruit salad using slices or chunks of peaches and nectarines. Peaches and nectarines are a good source of vitamin C.

Peach Raspberry Salad

MAKES 1 CUP

1 peach, peeled and diced
¼ cup raspberries
¼ cup vanilla yogurt

Gently mix peach, raspberries, and yogurt.

Pears

A very convenient food: All you need to do is remove the core. Just be sure the pear is really ripe, because an unripe pear has virtually no taste. After you remove the seeds, you can stuff the center with almond butter, reassemble, and wrap it snugly with plastic wrap.

Pears are a good source of fiber and vitamin C.

Pear Salad

MAKES 1 CUP

1 pear, peeled, seeded, and diced
1 tablespoon minced crystallized ginger
2 tablespoons reduced-fat sour cream

Gently mix pears, ginger, and sour cream.

Pineapple

You will have to peel and core and chop this pretty fruit before it is ready to eat, but often you can buy it already prepared in the supermarket. Either way, be sure that you remove all the little pieces of skin, because their sharp edges will make your mouth sore if you eat them. If you buy canned pineapple, be sure to get the variety that is packed in light (low sugar) syrup.

Pineapple is high in vitamin C.

Pineapple Salsa Salad

MAKES 1 CUP

1 cup pineapple chunks
¼ cup prepared salsa
1 tablespoon minced cilantro

Mix pineapple with salsa and cilantro.

Plums

The pits in plums are often not so easy to remove. The exception to this is the Italian prune plum, which does release its pit easily.

Plums are high in vitamin C.

Plum Salad

MAKES 1 CUP

3 plums, seeded and chunked
¼ cup low-fat yogurt
⅛ teaspoon ground cloves

Gently mix plums, yogurt, and cloves.

Fresh Fruit and Vegetable Kebabs

For a great presentation, skewer fruit chunks on a kebab stick. At work, seeing all these little ingredients on a stick is bound to cheer you up. You are also more likely to eat these combinations without a dressing, so you'll save some calories there. This is also great to bring to a potluck, because of its attractive presentation.

As you can see from the following suggestions, you can also make these kebabs with fruit and alternating pieces of cheese, hard salami, or cubed turkey breast. Fully cooked tortellini also can be skewered.

Combinations you might like to try:

Apples (dipped in lemon juice to keep from discoloring), cheddar cheese, and celery

Bananas, chicken, and jicama

Carrot, ham, and radishes

Cherries (remove the pits), salami, and cantaloupe

Cherry tomatoes, and tortellini

Cucumber, roasted lamb, and red pepper

Grapefruit sections, orange pieces, and peaches

Grapes, pineapple cubes, and strawberries

Honeydew melon and smoked ham (a classic appetizer combination served in the best restaurants)

Snow peas, water chestnuts, and roast pork

Turkey breast and mandarin orange pieces

Watermelon, honeydew melon, and beets

Zucchini, mild pepper jack cheese, and figs

Yogurt and Fruit

For a fraction of the cost of a store-bought small yogurt, you can put together a homemade one, reduce the sugar content, and increase the nutrition.

Be sure that your plain yogurt contains "live cultures." Check the label to make sure. These friendly bacteria actually protect the body against some of the infection-causing bacteria.

I use all-fruit spread instead of preserves or jam because it is perfectly sweet without the sugar of a jelly or jam. If you have been eating commercially sweetened yogurts, you might be used to a very sweet product, so try weaning yourself to a tarter taste little by little.

The frozen fruit in this recipe helps to keep the yogurt cold, but you can add fresh fruit too. Yogurt itself does not freeze well, but if you like to work ahead, you can freeze serving-size portions of frozen fruit and fruit spread.

MAKES 1⅓ CUPS

1 cup plain, natural, low-fat yogurt
3 tablespoons (more or less) peach all-fruit spread (no sugar added)
⅓ cup frozen peaches, cut into bite-size pieces

Mix the ingredients and place them into a plastic container with a well fitting top. Keep cold. Pack a frozen juice box or an ice pack with your lunch to keep the yogurt cold, and don't forget a spoon!

VARIATIONS: To have a "fruit at the bottom" yogurt lunch, spoon the fruit into the container first, place the preserves on top of that, and add the yogurt last.

Instead of the peach all-fruit spread, try any other all-fruit flavors such as strawberry, boysenberry, cherry, or apricot.

Instead of frozen peaches, try plums, cherries, or cut-up slices of mandarin oranges.

Pack ¼ cup granola in a separate container to sprinkle over the top of the yogurt. Keeping it separate prevents the granola from getting soggy.

If you have see-through serving containers, arrange the yogurt and fruit in alternating layers.

If you have a little plain cake left over, make a "trifle" by layering the cake in the middle.

Try combining cut-up apple, apple butter, and a sprinkle of cinnamon. Put the apple on the bottom to prevent browning.

Carrot Apple Salad

I dislike carrot salads made with mayonnaise: I just don't think it is a good combination. Try this simple salad, which you can make in a few minutes, and see if you don't agree that this is a tastier variation.

MAKES 2 CUPS

1 medium carrot, scraped
1 Granny Smith apple, peeled, cored, and quartered
1 tablespoon freshly squeezed lemon juice
1 tablespoon maple syrup

Using the grater blade in the food processor, grate the carrot and apple. Transfer the mixture to a bowl and sprinkle with the lemon juice and maple syrup. Mix well.

VARIATION: Instead of lemon juice and maple syrup, use 2 tablespoons of freshly squeezed orange juice.

Pear and Cottage Cheese

The texture and mild flavor of cottage cheese goes particularly well with pears, but you can substitute any fruit you like.

SERVES 2 TO 3

¾ cup cottage cheese

½ cup chopped celery

½ cup chopped pears

2 tablespoons raisins

¼ teaspoon ground cinnamon

Mix all the ingredients well.

VARIATIONS: Instead of celery and pear, use fruits such as apricots, strawberries, peaches, or halved seedless grapes.

Instead of raisins you can use other dried fruits.

cottagecheeseideas

If you like cottage cheese, fill a small container with a tight-fitting lid with the following combinations:

Cottage cheese, salad herbs

Cottage cheese, minced radish, red pepper, sprouts, sprinkle of dill

Cottage cheese, all-fruit preserves

Cottage cheese, pineapple rings, canned peaches, canned pears

Cottage cheese, peaches, pitted cherries or other fruits

Poached Pears

Anyone who tastes these pears will think you worked hard to make them, but it's a very easy recipe. And you'll have the added benefit of a delicious beverage from the poaching liquid.

SERVES 4

4 Seckel pears, halved and cored
2 cups water
¼ cup honey
1 teaspoon fresh lemon juice
2-inch strip of lemon zest
4 whole cloves
¼ teaspoon ground cinnamon

1. Place all ingredients in a saucepan and bring to a boil. Turn the heat down and simmer for 15 minutes. Let the pears cool in the poaching liquid.

2. Remove the pears from the poaching liquid only when you are ready to serve the pears. (Reserve the poaching liquid.)

3. To pack them for lunch, pack one or two halves in a plastic container. If you have them at home, you can either serve the pears warm with vanilla ice cream or at room temperature with vanilla yogurt.

VARIATION: *Pear Chai:* Combine ½ cup poaching liquid, 1 cup milk, and ⅛ teaspoon garam masala in a saucepan and bring to a boil. Remove the pan from the heat and hang 2 green-tea bags in the hot liquid for 5 minutes. Serve very warm.

Sweet Rice Salad

Sweet aromatic basmati, to my mind, is perfect for rice salad and rice pudding. You can, of course, also use other brown rice. Brown rice does take longer to cook, but the advantages in terms of the added fiber and the B vitamins are big enough that the time is worth your while.

MAKES 1 1/2 CUPS

1 cup cooked brown basmati rice

1/4 cup crushed, drained pineapple (reserve the juice)

1/4 cup raisins

1/4 cup chopped almonds

1 tablespoon pineapple juice

1 tablespoon low-fat yogurt

2 teaspoons mayonnaise

1. Place the rice, pineapple, raisins, and almonds in a bowl. Mix well.

2. In a separate dish, combine the pineapple juice, yogurt, and mayonnaise. When it is well blended, pour it over the rice mixture, and stir well. Chill to meld the flavors.

Desserts

The finishing touch to your lunch is a little something sweet. A cookie, a piece of cake, or a little rice pudding is very satisfying. If your lunch has been very filling you can save the dessert you packed for a midafternoon snack.

Sour Cream Cake

I have included this cake to prove to you that it is not necessary to buy baking mixes with questionable ingredients. With a little bit of planning, you can create a cake from scratch just as quickly.

Making a cake in a food processor is a baking contest no-no, because the cake batter is easily overblended and, therefore, the cake rises in the middle. But I have designed these recipes to be fast and easy, and I can't imagine that the shape of the cake makes any difference at all.

This cake is rich and sweet and a small slice goes a long way. It's good with mashed, unsweetened strawberries on top.

MAKES 1 CAKE

1 cup white sugar
½ cup light brown sugar
5 tablespoons butter, cut in
    pieces
¾ cup reduced-fat sour cream
3 eggs

1 cup unbleached all-purpose
    flour
1¼ cups whole wheat flour
½ teaspoon baking soda
1 teaspoon almond extract
1 teaspoon vanilla extract

1. Preheat the oven to 325°F. Grease a 9-by-9-inch baking pan.

2. Put the sugars and butter in a food processor fitted with the steel blade. Blend until very smooth.

3. Add the sour cream and eggs and blend well. Add the flours, baking soda, and extracts. Blend until the batter is just smooth.

4. Pour the batter into the prepared pan. Bake for 50 minutes or until a wooden toothpick inserted in the middle comes out clean. Cool in the pan for 20 minutes before removing.

Gingerbread

This treat is practically fat-free, so it provides a good balance for a meal with high-fat foods. Because I like the recipe a lot, I keep a little jar with the spices premixed in them (I just keep the same proportions). Then I can easily measure out 1½ teaspoons each time I want to make gingerbread.

MAKES 9 LARGE PIECES

1½ cups whole wheat flour

⅔ cup light brown sugar

1 teaspoon baking soda

½ teaspoon baking powder

1 teaspoon ground ginger

¼ teaspoon ground cloves

¼ teaspoon ground cinnamon

2 eggs

⅓ cup applesauce

⅓ cup water

½ teaspoon apple cider vinegar

1. Preheat the oven to 300°F. Grease a 9-by-9-inch baking pan.

2. In a large bowl combine the flour, sugar, baking soda, baking powder, ginger, cloves, and cinnamon.

3. In a separate bowl combine the eggs, applesauce, water, and vinegar.

4. Add the liquid ingredients to the flour mixture and combine lightly but thoroughly. Pour the batter into the prepared pan and smooth out. Bake for 25 minutes or until a wooden toothpick inserted near the center comes out clean.

5. Let the gingerbread cool in the pan for 10 minutes before removing it from the pan. Serve warm or cool.

Cranberry Upside-Down Cake

I brought this cake to a Christmas gathering and it was a huge success. The jewel-like cranberries end up on top and the cake is delicious. You can also place the traditional pineapple on the bottom of the pan. It is a sweet cake, so a little goes a long way.

MAKES 15 PIECES

1 tablespoon unsalted butter

1 cup light brown sugar

4 cups cranberries, frozen or fresh, washed and picked over

2½ cups unbleached all-purpose flour

1½ cups brown sugar

3 teaspoons baking powder

Zest from 1 lemon

1 cup low-fat milk

2 eggs

½ cup applesauce

¼ cup extra-light-tasting olive oil

½ teaspoon vanilla extract

¼ teaspoon lemon extract

1. Preheat the oven to 350°F. Generously grease a 9-by-13-inch baking pan.

2. Sprinkle ½ cup of the brown sugar over the pan. Sprinkle the cranberries over that and top with the remaining ½ cup of sugar. Cover the pan tightly with aluminum foil. Bake the berries for 30 minutes. Take the pan out of the oven and remove the foil carefully (steam will escape).

3. Meanwhile, put the flour, 1½ cups of brown sugar, baking powder, and lemon zest in a food processor fitted with the steel blade. Process until well blended.

4. Add the milk, eggs, applesauce, oil, and extracts. Let the food processor run for 1 minute, scraping the sides down occasionally. Spoon the batter over the cranberries and smooth out gently.

5. Bake the cake for 35 to 45 minutes, or until a wooden toothpick inserted in the center comes out clean.

6. Remove the cake from the oven and run a spatula around the edge. Invert the cake onto a serving plate, leaving the pan over the cake for a few minutes. Serve hot, warm, or cold.

VARIATION: *Almond Cranberry Upside-Down Cake:* After the cranberries are baked, sprinkle ¼ cup slivered almonds over them, before pouring in the batter. Omit the lemon zest and replace the lemon extract with ½ teaspoon of almond extract.

One-Pan Cake

With a recipe like this, you can't say it's too hard to make a cake! This cake takes just minutes to make, and only one pan and a few measuring spoons and cups ever get dirty. Its other advantage is that the ingredients are generally available in your home. If you serve it at home, top it with a scoop of ice cream.

MAKES 1 CAKE

1¼ cups whole wheat flour
1 cup light brown sugar
¼ cup oat bran
3 tablespoons cocoa powder
1 tablespoon dry nonfat milk powder
1 teaspoon baking soda
¼ teaspoon salt
6 tablespoons extra-light-tasting olive oil
1 tablespoon apple cider vinegar
1 teaspoon vanilla extract
1 cup low-fat milk or water

1. Preheat the oven to 350°F.

2. Mix the flour, sugar, bran, cocoa powder, milk powder, baking soda and salt in an ungreased 9-by-9-inch baking pan. Make sure all the ingredients are well distributed.

3. Make three wells in the flour mixture. Pour the oil in one well, the vinegar in another, and the vanilla in the third. Pour the milk over all. Mix everything well. If you are using a nonstick pan, you might like to use a plastic spoon so you don't gouge it.

4. Bake for 30 minutes or until a wooden toothpick inserted in the middle comes out clean. Let cake cool in the pan about 10 minutes before slicing.

Zucchini Chocolate Cake

It is rare that you can get a bit of vegetable in a swee[t]
zucchini breads are filled with lots of oil, which makes them surprisingly high in calories. Not this delicious cake.

MAKES 1 CAKE

1 small zucchini

1 cup whole wheat flour

1 cup unbleached all-purpose
   flour

1 cup light brown sugar

¼ cup cocoa powder

4 tablespoons dry buttermilk
   powder

1 teaspoon baking powder

1 teaspoon baking soda

½ teaspoon salt

1 cup water

⅓ cup extra-light-tasting olive
   oil

1 egg

⅓ cup walnut halves *(no)*

½ c choc. chips)

yum!
2/5/16

1. Preheat oven to 375°F. Grease and flour a 9-by-9-inch pan.

2. Place the grating disc in the food processor, and grate the zucchini. Measure 1 cup and place the zucchini in a colander and let
   it drip for 15 minutes.

3. In a large mixing bowl, mix together the whole wheat flour, white
   flour, sugar, cocoa, buttermilk powder, baking powder, baking
   soda, and salt and mix well.

4. Put the water, oil, and egg in a medium bowl and mix well. Add
   the zucchini and stir well.

5. Combine the zucchini mixture with the flour mixture and blend
   with long gentle strokes until just mixed. Spread the batter in the
   pan and smooth the top. Sprinkle the walnuts on top.

6. Bake for 45 minutes or until a toothpick inserted in the center
   comes out clean. Let the cake cool in the pan before slicing.

Apple Pie-Cake

When I brought this dessert to a potluck, it got rave reviews. You might not think there are enough wet ingredients in the recipe to make a batter, but it works surprisingly well.

SERVES 6

1 egg
¾ cup light brown sugar
1½ teaspoons vanilla extract
4 apples, peeled, cored, and chopped
½ cup whole wheat flour
¼ teaspoon ground cinnamon
1 teaspoon baking powder
Pinch of salt

1. Preheat the oven to 350°F. Butter a pie plate.

2. Beat the egg in a bowl. Add the sugar and vanilla extract and mix well. Add the apples and mix well. Add the flour, cinnamon, baking powder, and salt. Mix well.

3. Put the batter in the prepared pie plate, spread it around evenly, and bake for 25 to 30 minutes. Let the cake cool in the pan for 10 minutes before slicing.

Apple Crisp

It's so easy to make a fruit crisp that you should always think about making extra. That way you can take a serving to work the next day. It is just as delicious cold as it is hot.

SERVES 6

6 to 8 apples, peeled, cored, and sliced
⅔ cup light brown sugar
½ cup whole wheat flour
½ cup rolled oats
½ teaspoon ground cinnamon
¼ teaspoon ground cloves
⅓ cup unsalted butter, softened, in pieces

1. Preheat oven to 375°F. Grease a shallow 1½-quart casserole.

2. Layer the apples in the casserole.

3. Put the sugar, flour, oats, cinnamon, and cloves in a food processor fitted with a steel blade. Process until the oatmeal flakes are about half their original size.

4. Add the softened butter to the sugar-flour mixture and blend well. Sprinkle the mixture over the apples. If the mixture is in a large ball, just drop the batter a tablespoon at a time over the apples.

5. Bake for about 30 minutes. Serve hot, warm, or cold. If transporting it, you will need a plastic container with a secure cover.

VARIATIONS: Almost all fruits can go into a crisp, but remember that if you use berries, the result will be a little more mushy. Other fruits to try alone or in combination, are peaches, pears, apricots, blueberries, or plums.

You can sprinkle a few raisins or other little pieces of dried fruits over the crisp.

Apple Squares

This makes a lot of dessert, so it is perfect to bring along for a potluck or an office party. If you like these squares, you can also experiment with other fruits as well. Peaches and apricots work especially well, but if you use blueberries be sure to omit the raisins.

Instead of the dry milk and water, you can add a little more than $\frac{2}{3}$ cup of milk.

MAKES 18 SQUARES

½ cup whole wheat flour	1 egg
½ cup unbleached all-purpose flour	⅔ cup water
½ cup light brown sugar	3 medium apples, peeled and sliced
⅓ cup nonfat dry milk powder	⅓ cup raisins
1 teaspoon baking powder	¼ cup light brown sugar
¼ teaspoon ground cloves	1 teaspoon ground cinnamon
Pinch salt	

1. Preheat the oven to 350°F. Grease a 9-by-13-inch baking pan and set aside.

2. In a large bowl combine the whole wheat flour, white flour, ½ cup brown sugar, milk powder, baking powder, cloves, and salt and mix well.

3. In a small bowl mix the egg and water. Add it to the flour mixture. Blend well.

4. Pour the batter in the prepared pan and spread the batter evenly.

5. Place the apples over the batter (in rows or another nice pattern) and sprinkle the raisins over the top.

6. In a small bowl mix the ¼ cup brown sugar and cinnamon. Sprinkle the sugar mixture over the apples and batter. Bake for 35 minutes or until a wooden toothpick inserted in the middle comes out clean. Let cool in pan before slicing into squares.

Bread Pudding

Talk about comfort food! This is one of my favorite desserts to make and eat. If you use whole grain bread, you'll get a fair amount of fiber.

SERVES 9

6 slices stale whole grain bread
1 cup low-fat milk
2 eggs
⅓ cup light brown sugar
1 teaspoon vanilla extract
½ teaspoon ground cinnamon
¼ cup raisins

1. Preheat the oven to 350°F. Butter a 9-by-9-inch baking pan.

2. Tear the bread into small, 1-inch-square pieces in a large bowl. Pour the milk over the bread and let it stand for 30 minutes.

3. Put the eggs, sugar, vanilla, and cinnamon into another bowl. Mix well. Pour over the soaked bread. Sprinkle the raisins over all and mix well.

4. Pour the bread mixture into the prepared pan, and spread it out evenly. Bake the bread pudding for 30 minutes.

5. Serve hot, warm, or cold.

Rice Pudding

This recipe makes about two servings, but you can double or triple the amounts with no problem. You will end up with a very creamy pudding, which will become stiff when cold, and, therefore, will transport easily for lunch in a tightly closed container.

I use basmati rice because its delicious taste beats plain white rice by a mile.

SERVES 2

½ cup white basmati rice

1 cup water

1 cup 2 percent milk

¼ teaspoon vanilla extract

⅛ teaspoon almond extract

3 tablespoons light brown sugar

1. In a small saucepan bring the rice, water, and milk to a boil over gentle heat. Turn down the heat and simmer, uncovered, for 20 to 25 minutes, stirring frequently to prevent scorching.

2. Remove the pan from the heat. Immediately add the vanilla and almond extracts and stir well. Stir in the sugar and mix well.

3. Serve hot, warm, or cool.

Carole's Cookies

These are truly the best, healthiest, easiest-to-make cookies, and I have my friend Carole Owens to thank for the recipe. No matter what tale of woe I have to tell her, these cookies, a cup of tea, and her sage advice are guaranteed to help me gain a new perspective on life.

MAKES 12 COOKIES

1 cup rolled oats (not instant)
1 cup whole wheat flour
1 cup walnuts
½ cup extra-light-tasting olive oil
½ cup maple syrup
Pinch salt

1. Preheat the oven to 375°F. Take out a large cookie sheet.

2. Put the oats in a food processor fitted with a steel blade. Pulse on/off until the oats are in small pieces. There will still be little pieces of oats visible, which will give the finished cookie a nice chewy texture.

3. Add the flour and process. Add the walnuts, oil, maple syrup, vanilla, and salt and run the food processor until everything is well mixed.

4. Drop the batter on the cookie sheet, a generous tablespoon per cookie. Bake for 12 minutes. Remove the cookies and let them cool on a plate. Freeze leftovers. You can let the cookies thaw on their own, or warm them up in a microwave for a fresh-baked sensation.

VARIATION: While the cookie is cooling, you can make a little well in the top by pushing a small teaspoon into the center. Fill the depression with a little all-fruit spread.

Kugel

Traditionally this dish is made with egg noodles, but you can use any kind of cooked pasta. If you have a lot of leftover pasta, you can easily double the recipe.

SERVES 2

1 cup light sour cream

1 egg

¼ cup reduced-fat cream cheese

¼ cup light brown sugar

1 teaspoon vanilla extract

1 cup cooked noodles

¼ cup golden raisins

1. Preheat the oven to 350°F. Grease a 1½-quart dish.

2. In a blender combine the sour cream, egg, cream cheese, sugar, and vanilla. Blend until smooth.

3. In a large bowl combine the sour cream mixture, noodles, and raisins. Spoon into the prepared dish. Bake for 50 minutes.

4. Serve hot, warm, or cold.

Index

About the Author

Miriam Jacobs was born in Montevideo of Dutch parents. By the time she was a young adult, she had lived in urban Uruguay, rural India, on a kibbutz in Israel, and at home in Holland. She came to America and settled in New York City, where she graduated from Brooklyn College with a major in dance.

Adapting quickly to the United States, Miriam fell temporarily in love with fast food; for balance, she swallowed lots of vitamin pills. Her first true culinary inspiration came from *The Vegetarian Epicure* by Anna Thomas, and by making her first authentic Canard a l'Orange. Miriam then taught herself to cook by reading shelffuls of cookbooks and by trying many cuisines and dishes. Now, decades later, having collected hundreds of cookbooks, she is still known to find holes in her collection and to need to acquire "just one more" cookbook.

Miriam raised and fed her three children, Sarah, Abigail, and Adam, in the Berkshire Hills in western Massachusetts. She wrote recipe, food history, and cookbook review columns for a decade for two Berkshire regional publications, *Homestyle* magazine and the *Independent* newspaper. For Berkshire House Publishers, Miriam wrote *Best Recipes of Berkshire Chefs* and did the recipe testing for *The Red Lion Inn Cookbook*. For Storey Publishing, Miriam wrote *The 10% Low Fat Cookbook, Cooking with Soy,* and *Cooking With Edible Flowers*. She is also the author of *The School Lunchbox Cookbook* (Globe Pequot).

Lately her writing has turned to murder mysteries and travel writing.

Miriam now lives on the Gulf Coast in Florida, where she walks on the beach, samples fresh fish, and continues to cook new things.